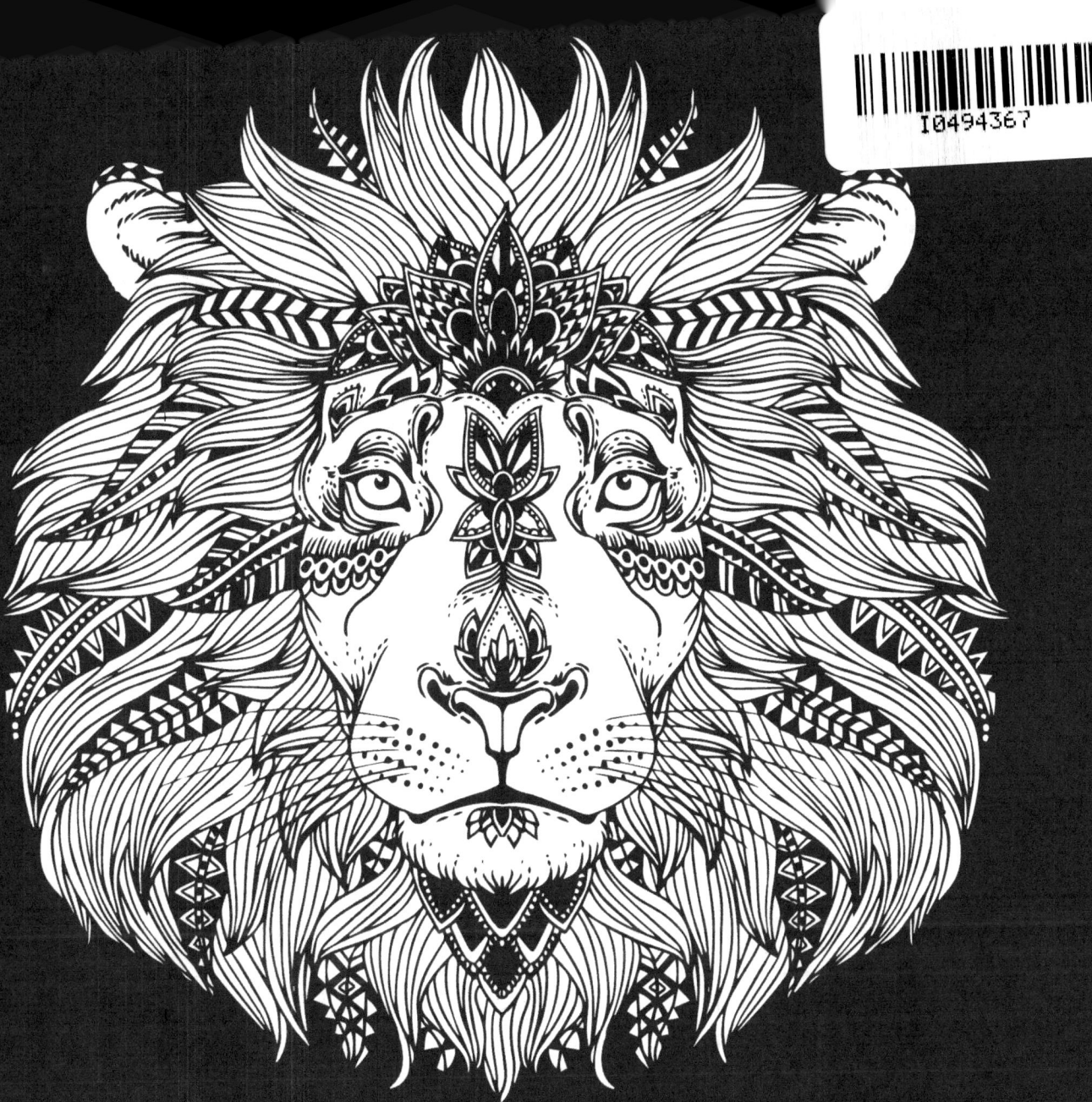

LION
COLORING BOOK
FOR ADULTS

ART THERAPY COLORING

Preview of Coloring Pages

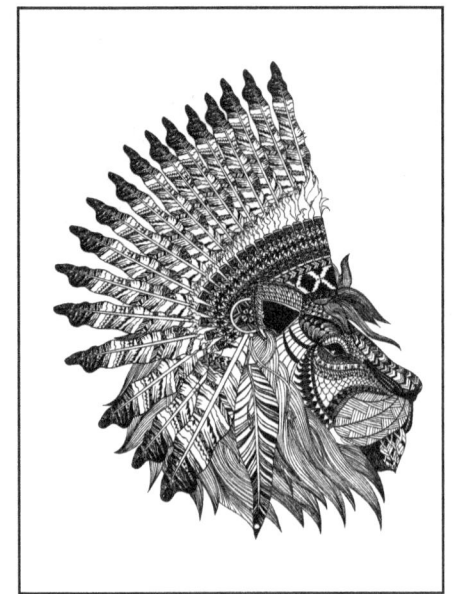
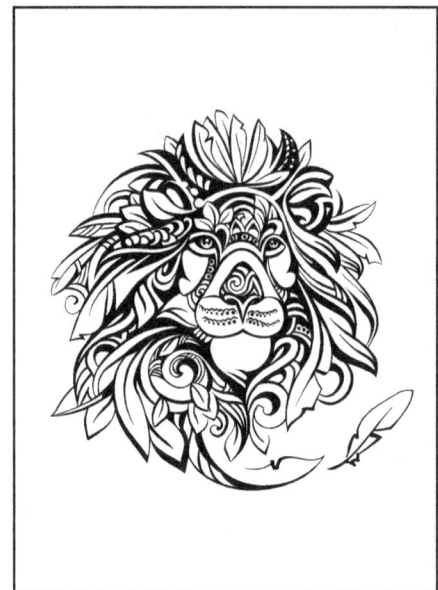
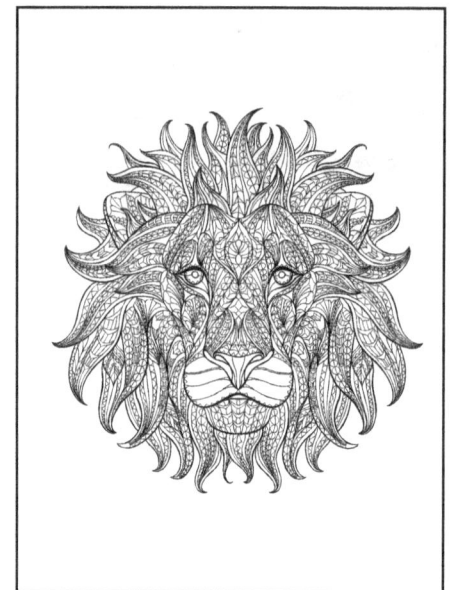
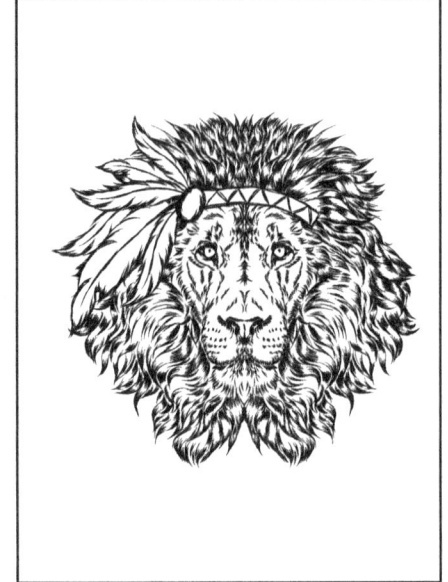
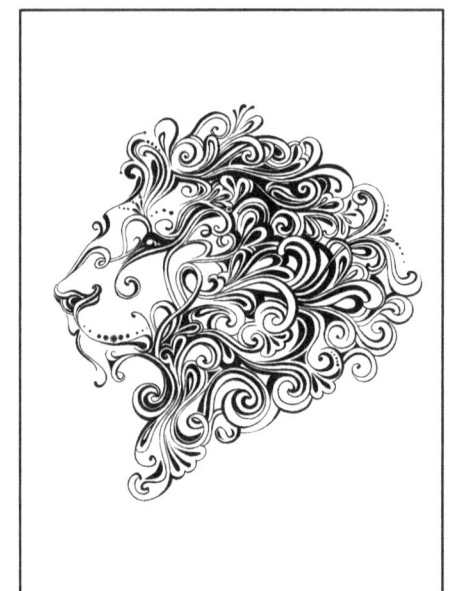
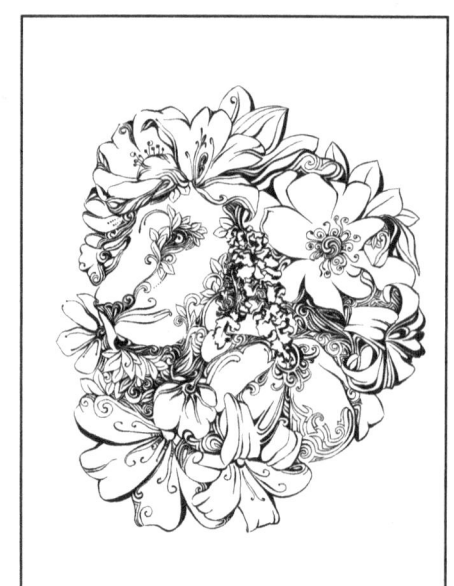
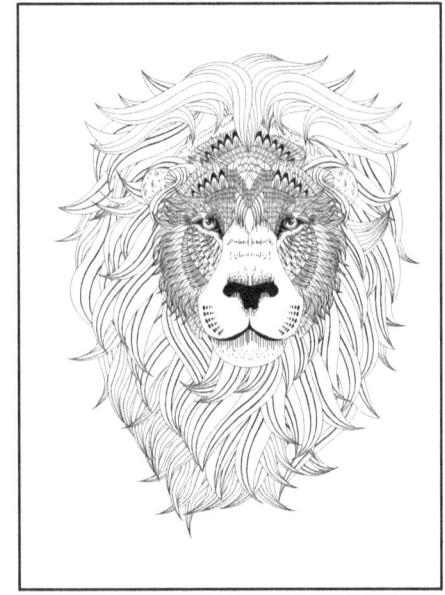
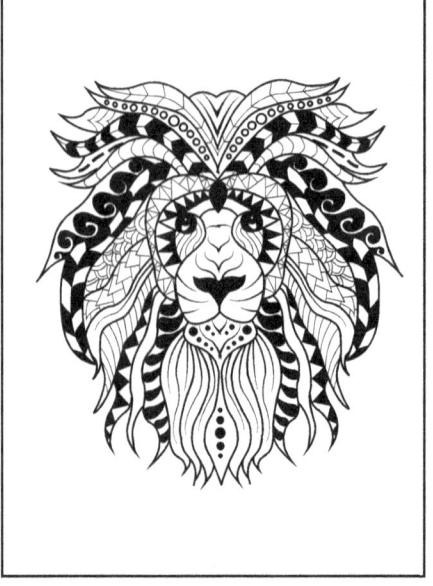
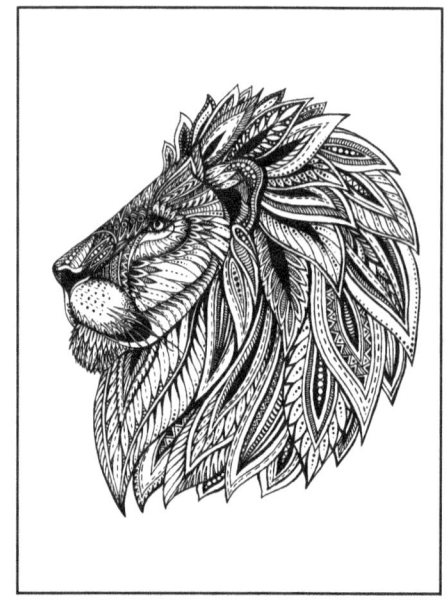

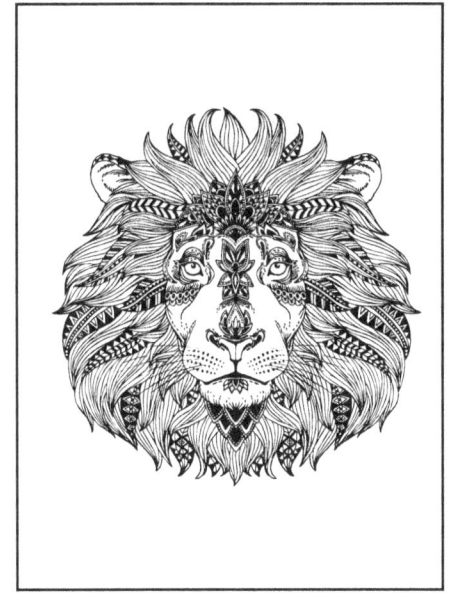
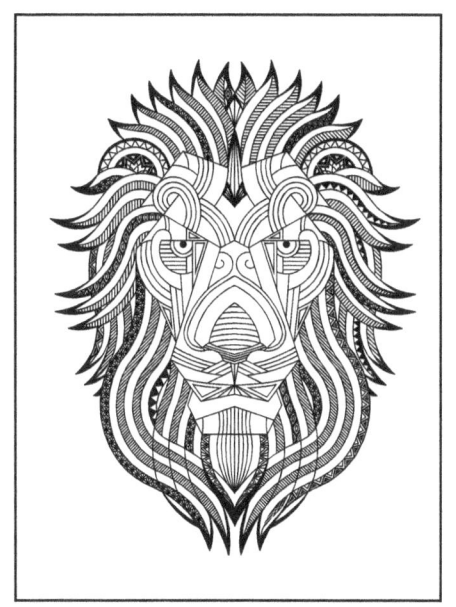
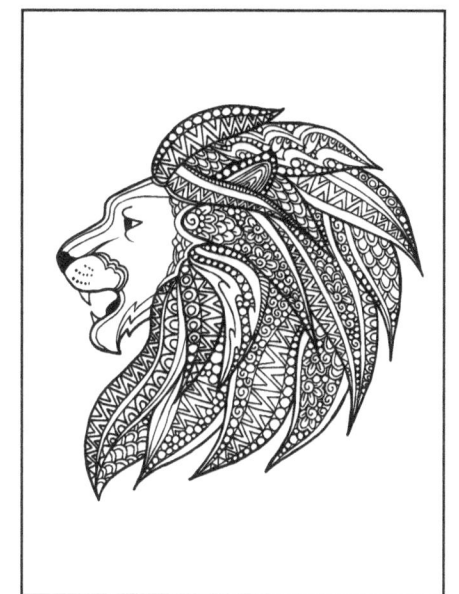
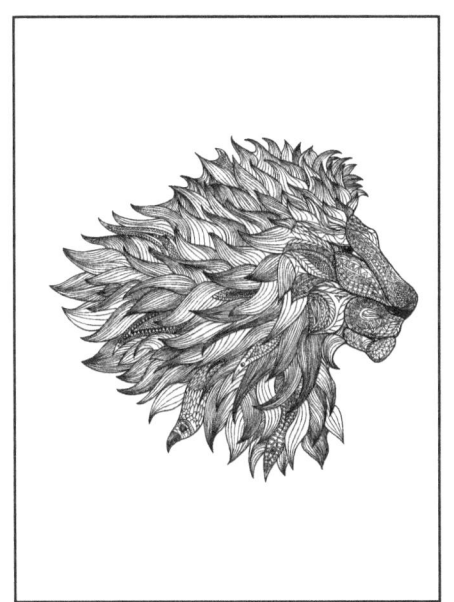
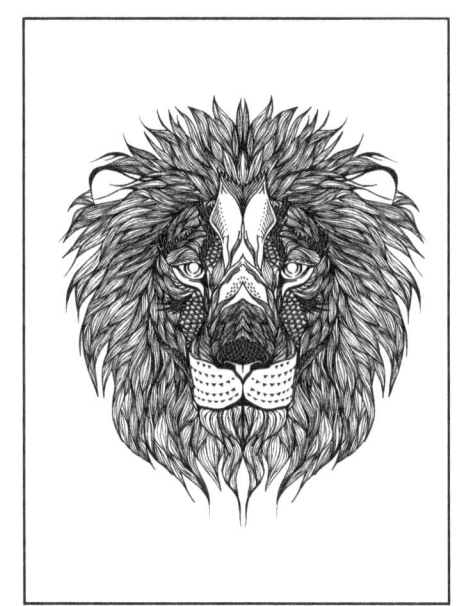
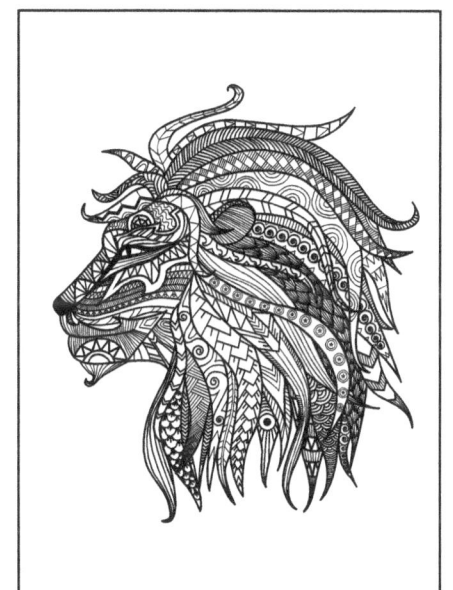
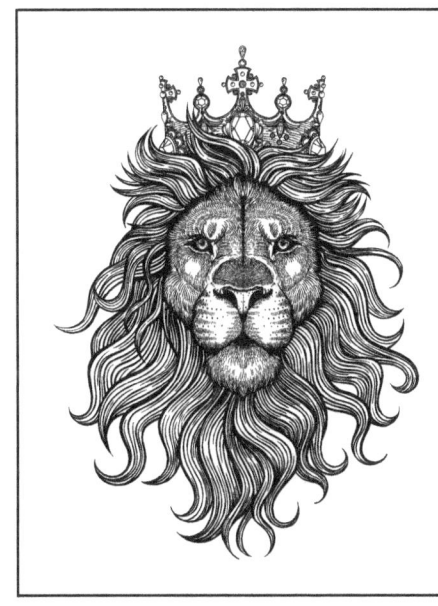
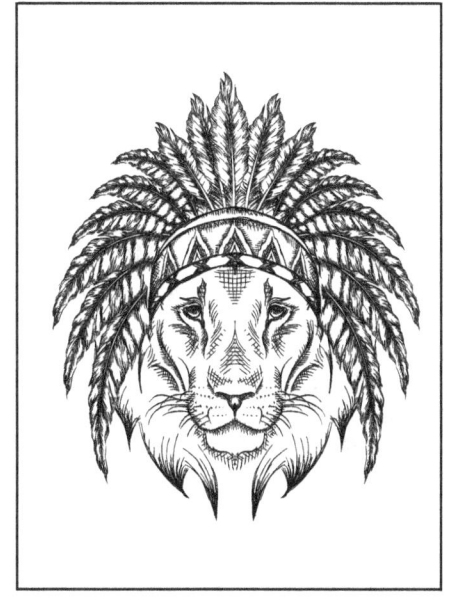
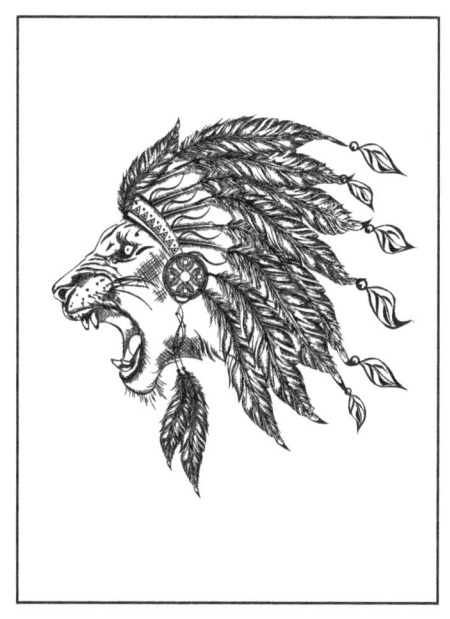

Preview of Coloring Pages

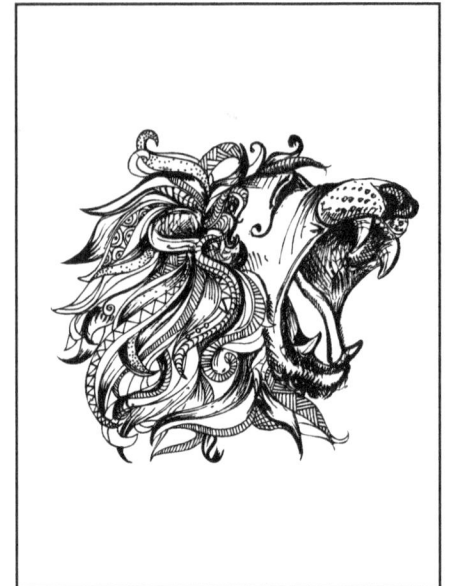
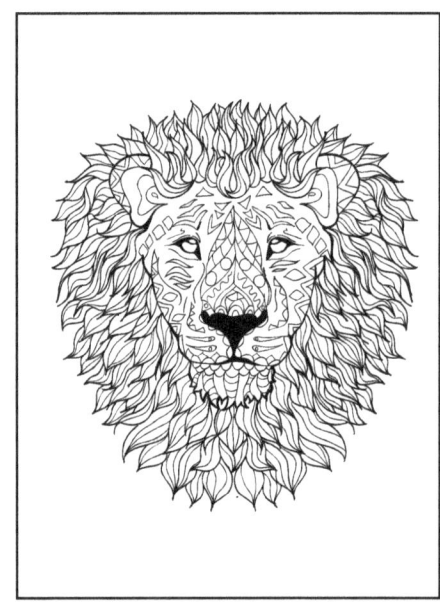
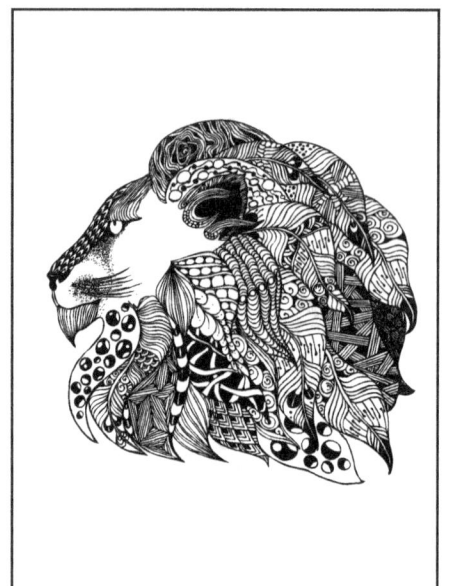
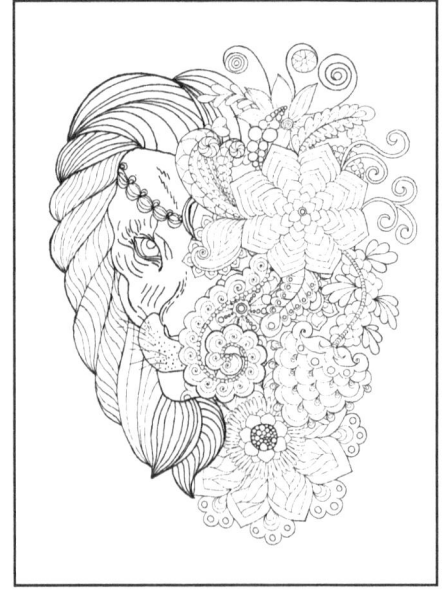
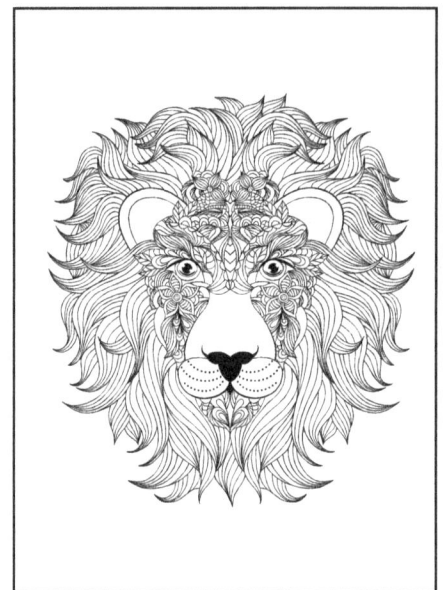
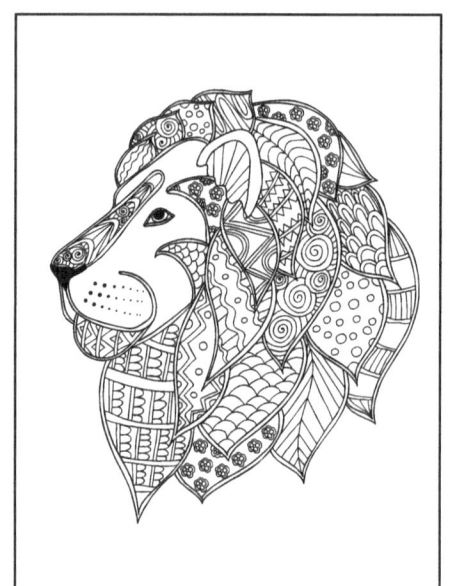
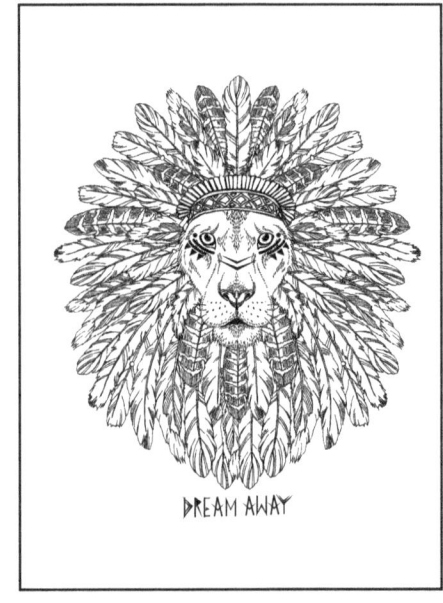
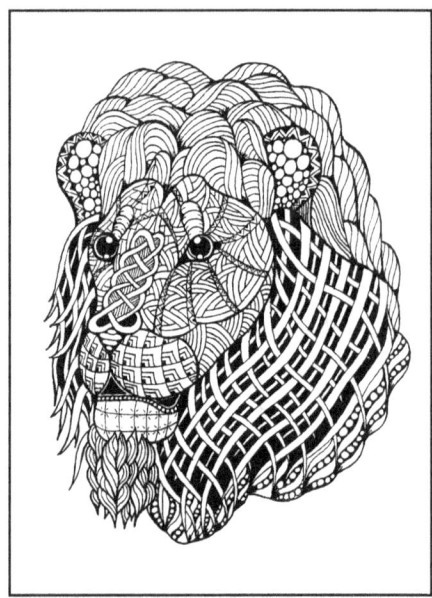
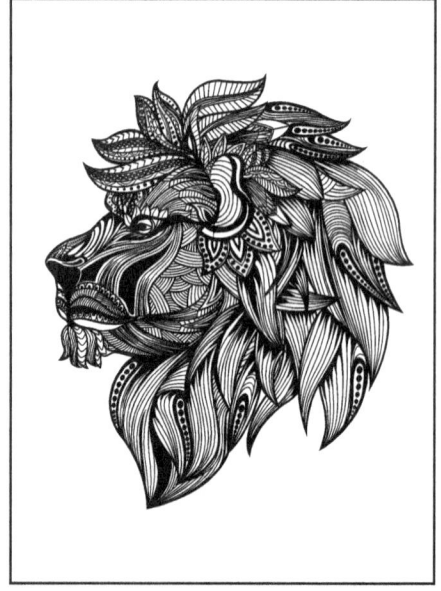

DREAM AWAY

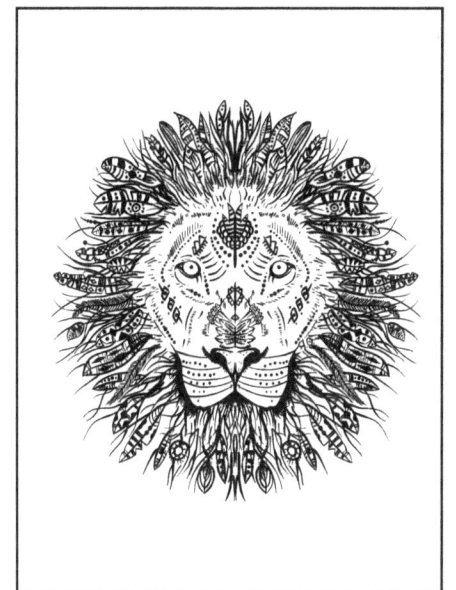
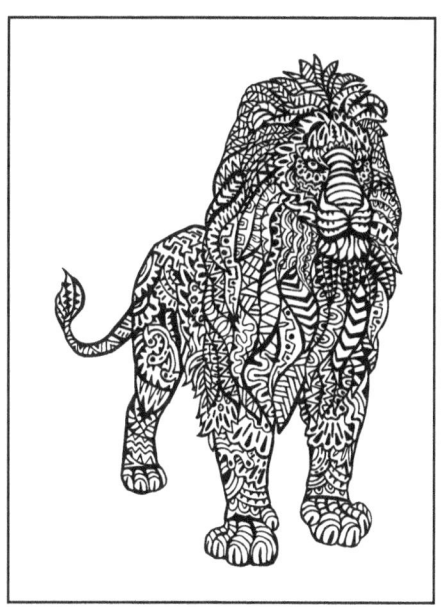
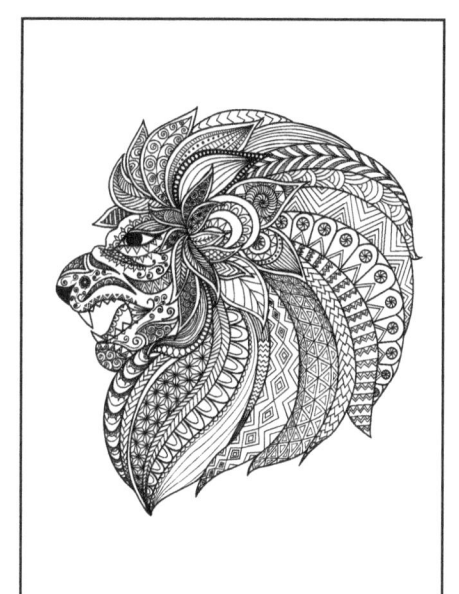
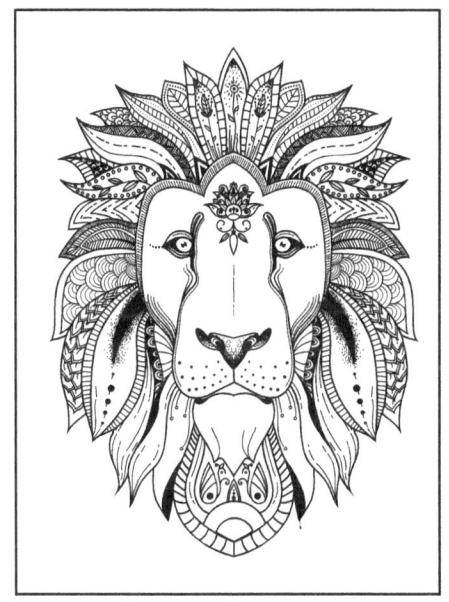
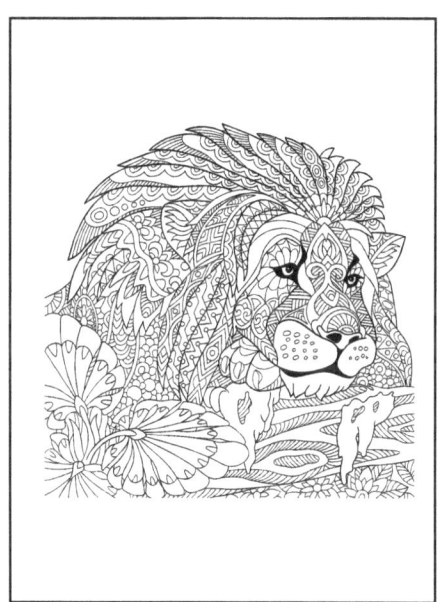
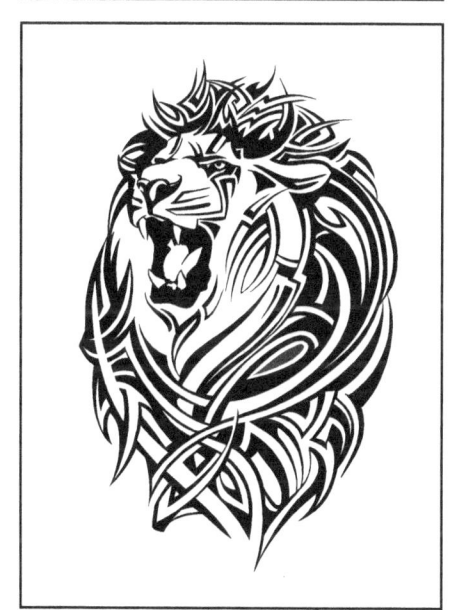
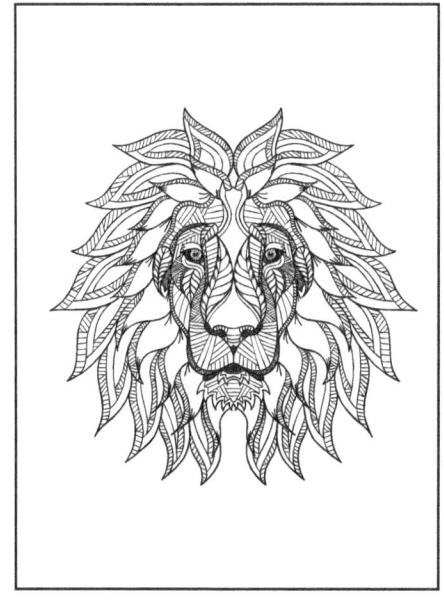
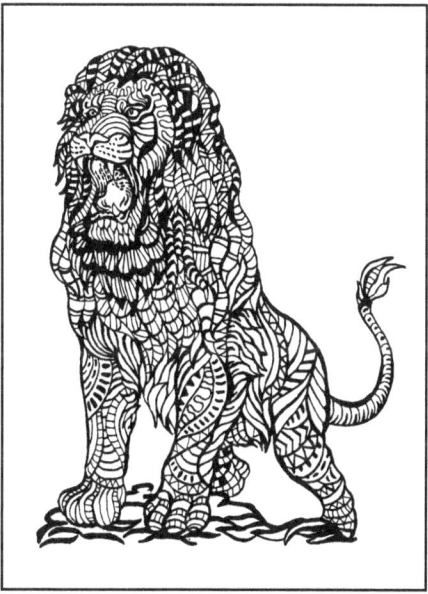
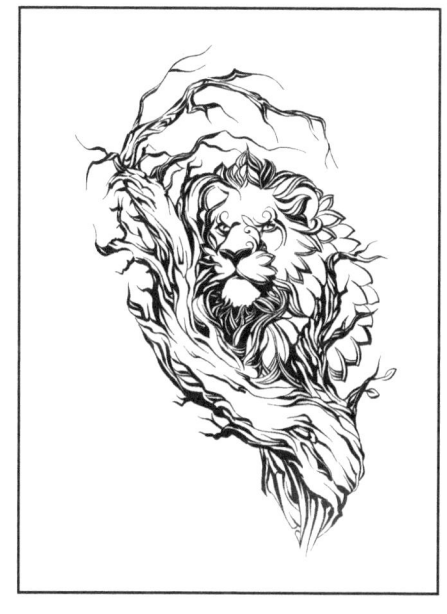

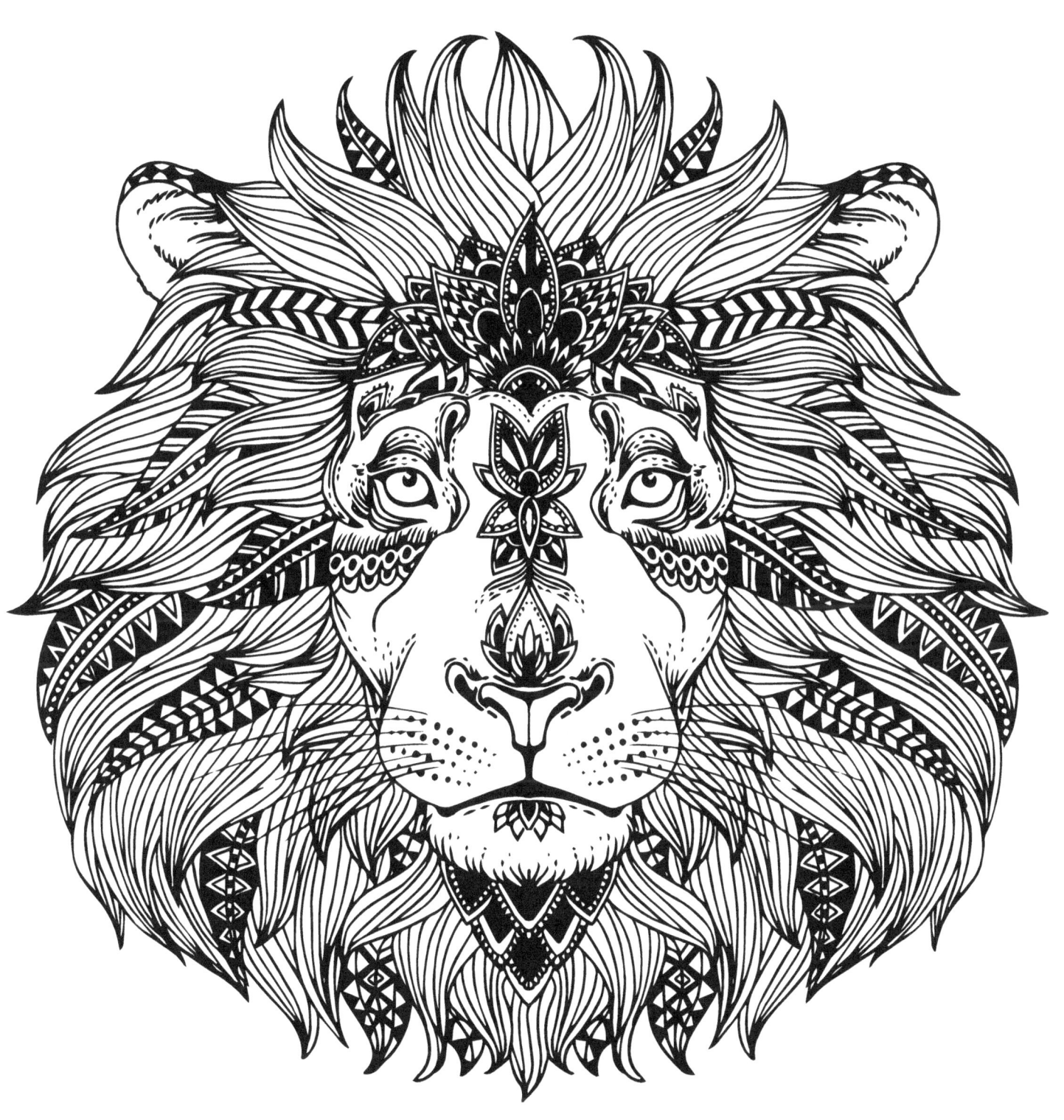

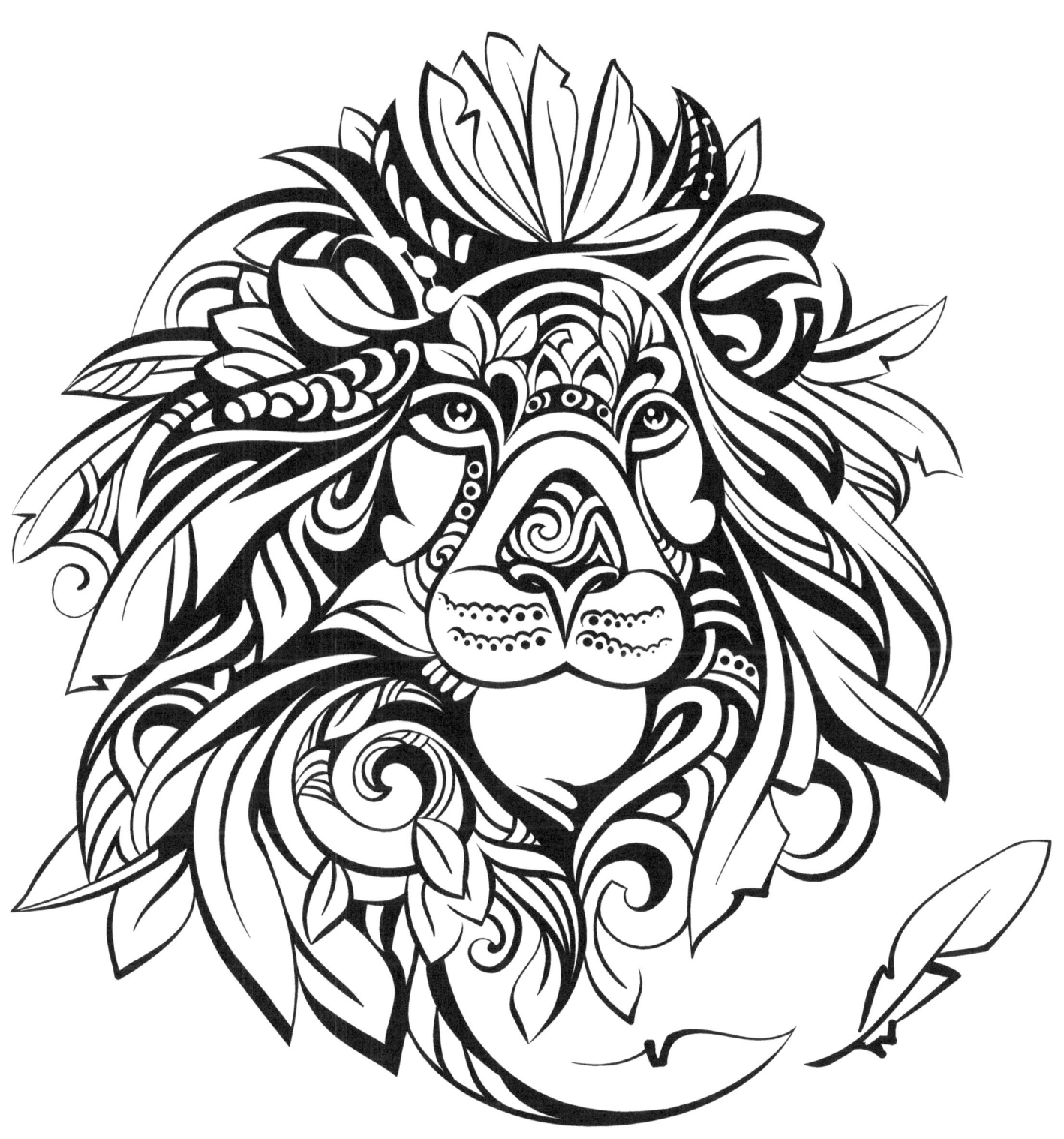

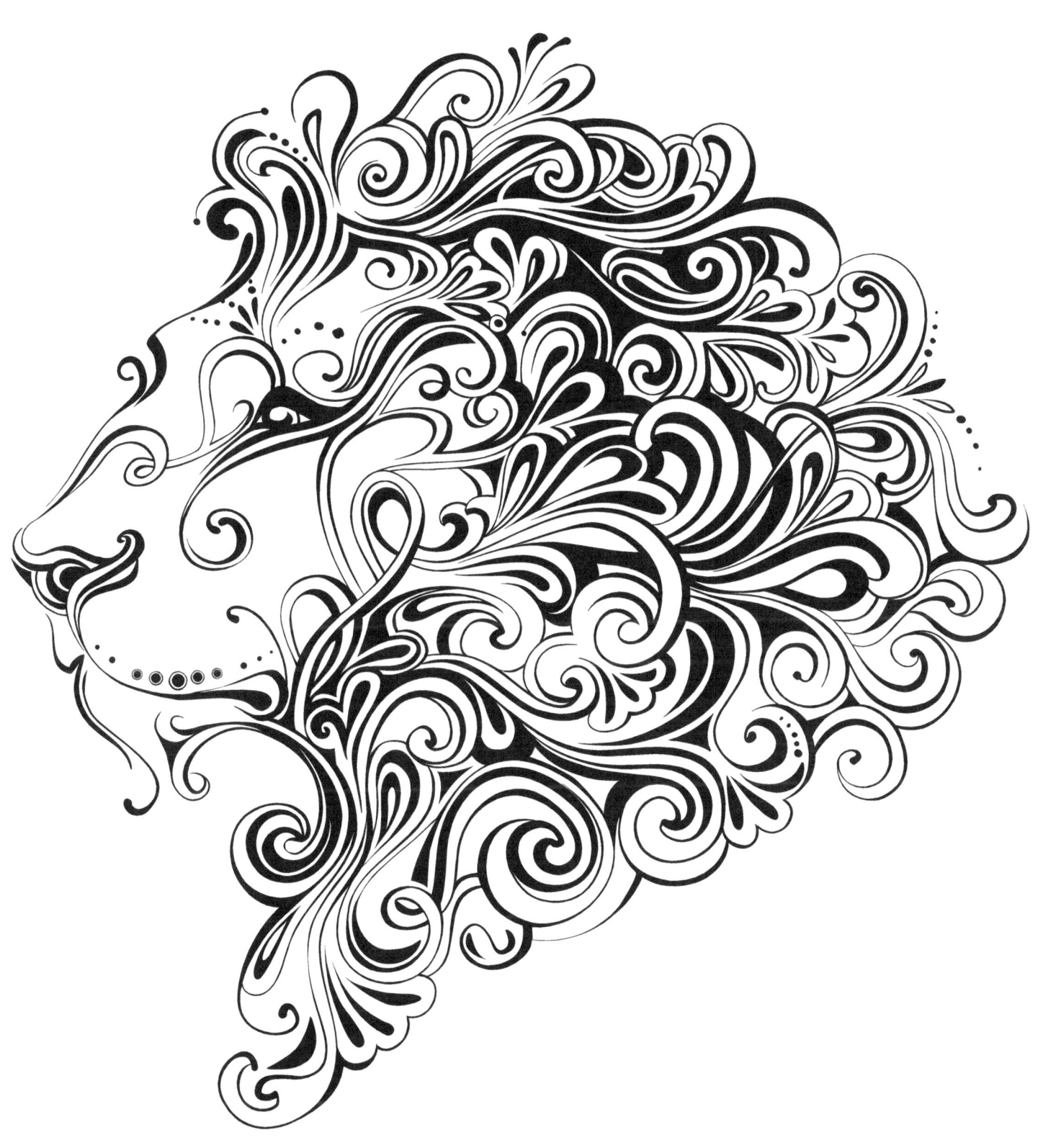

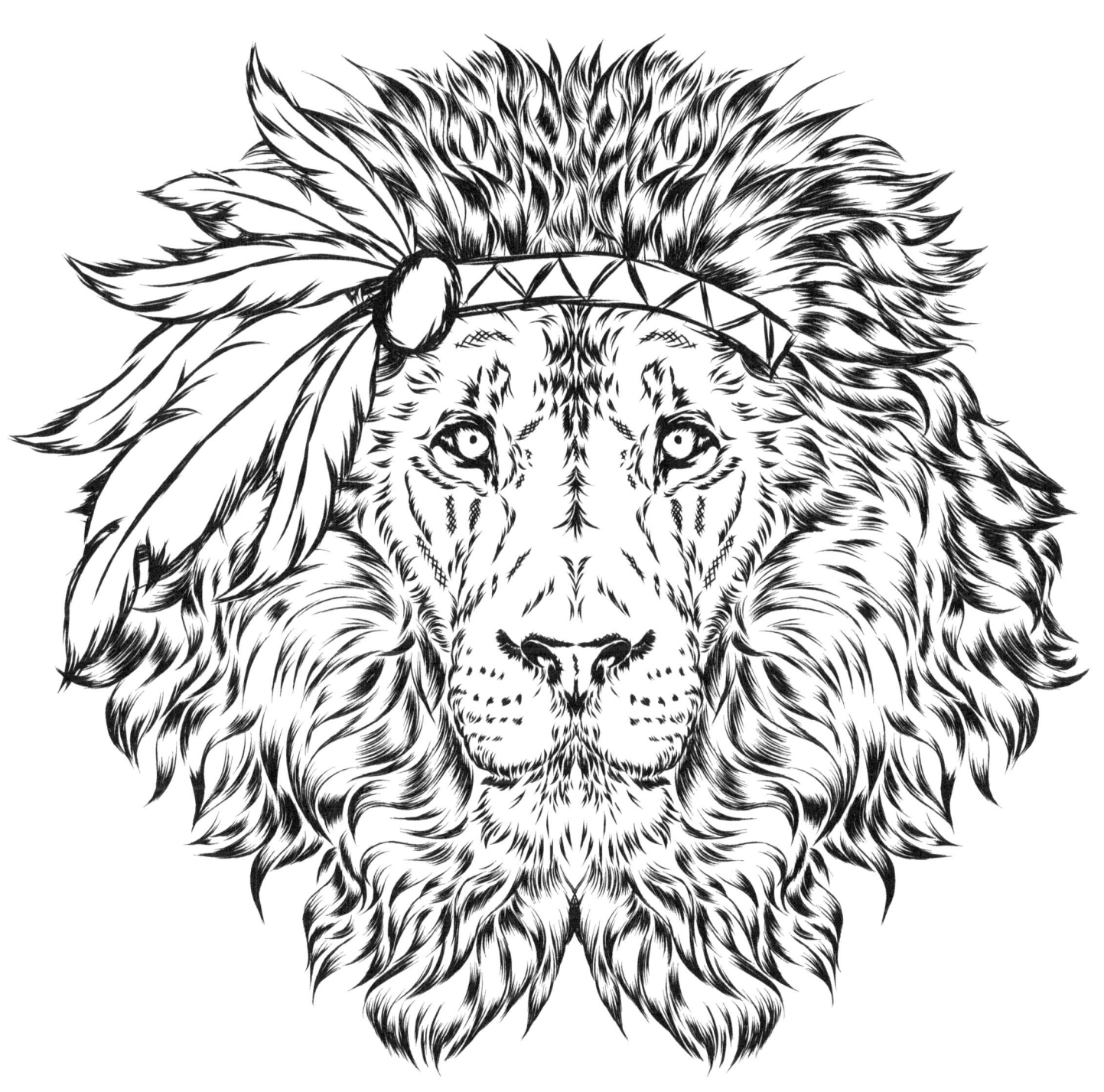

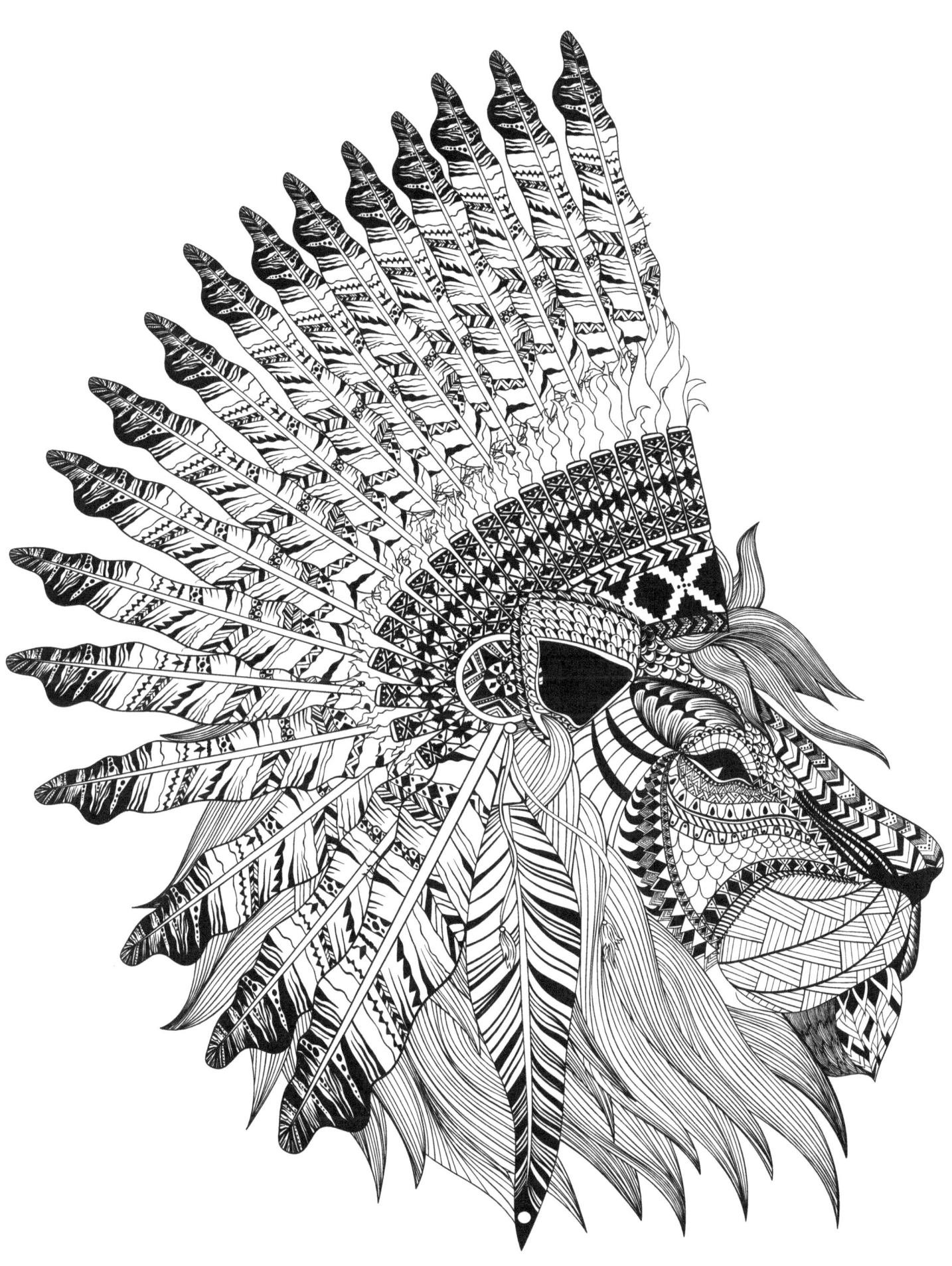

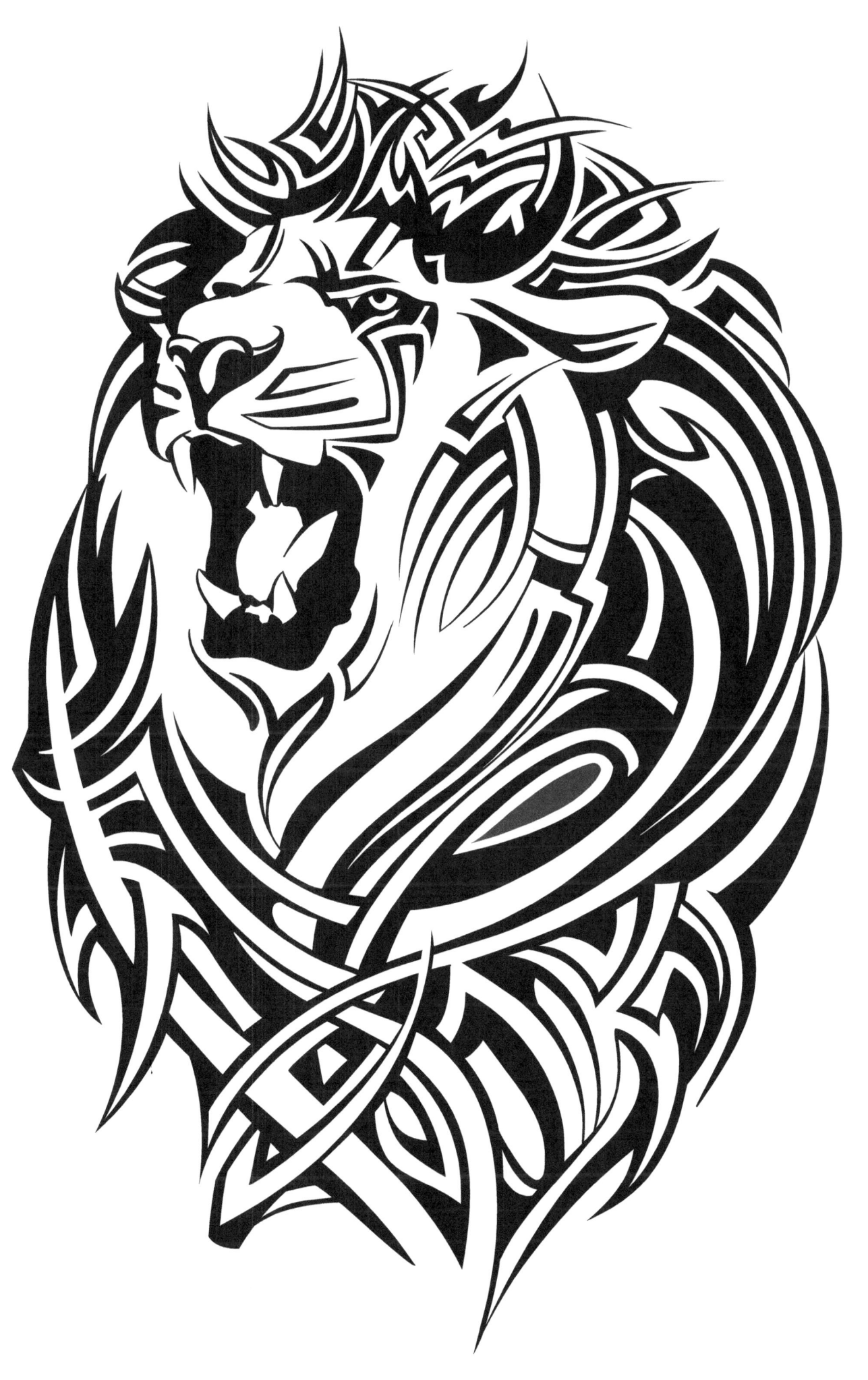

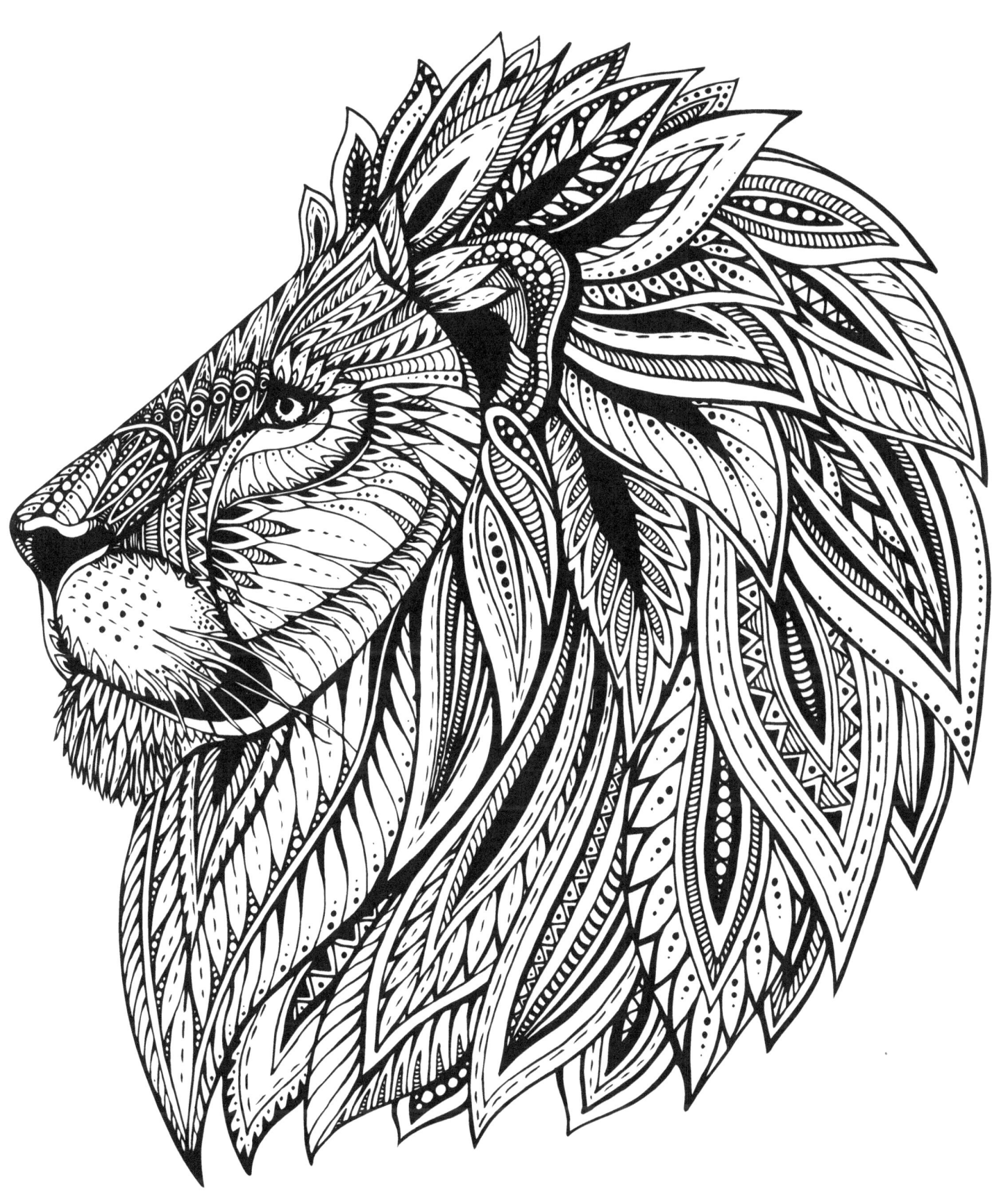

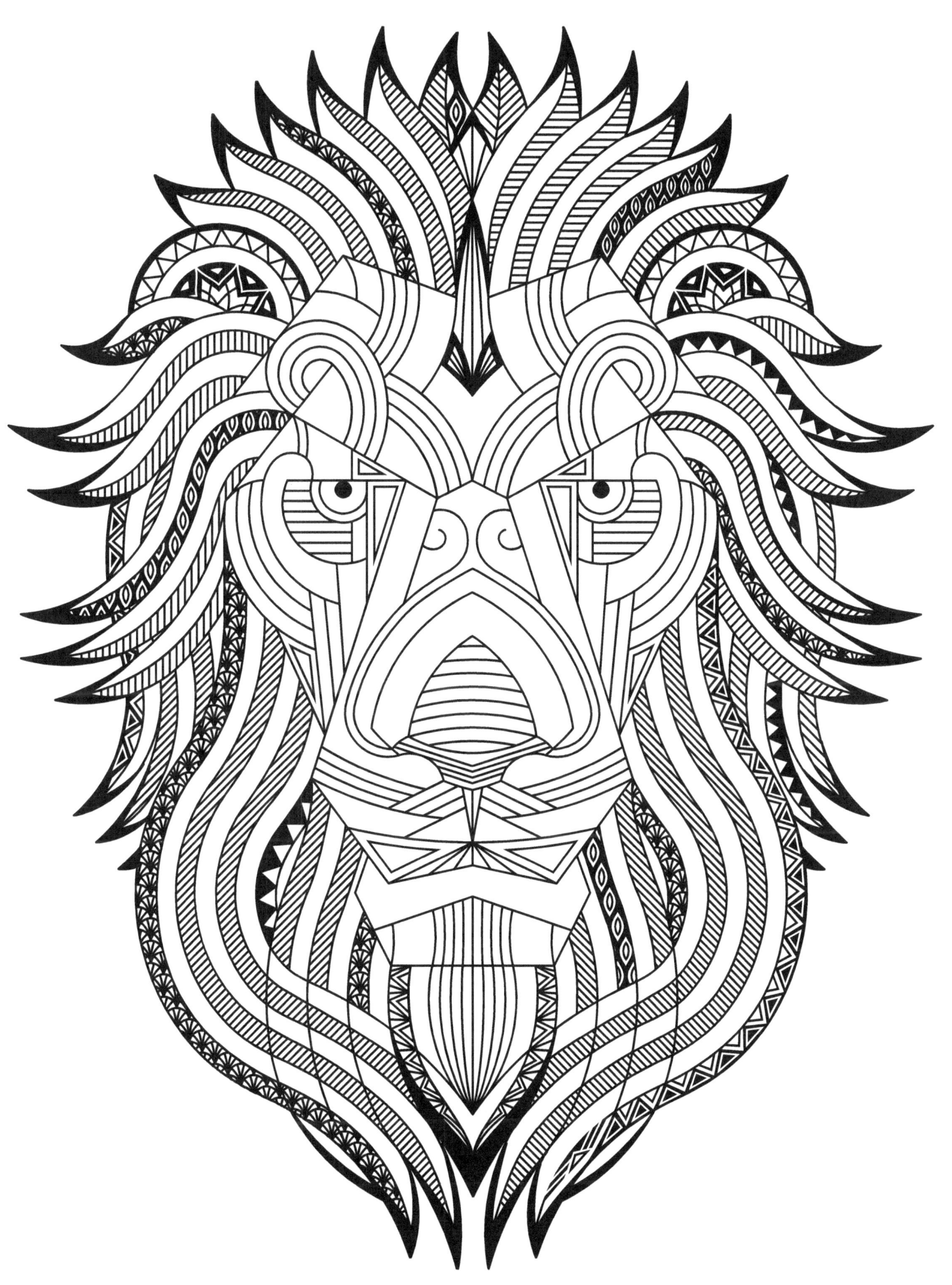

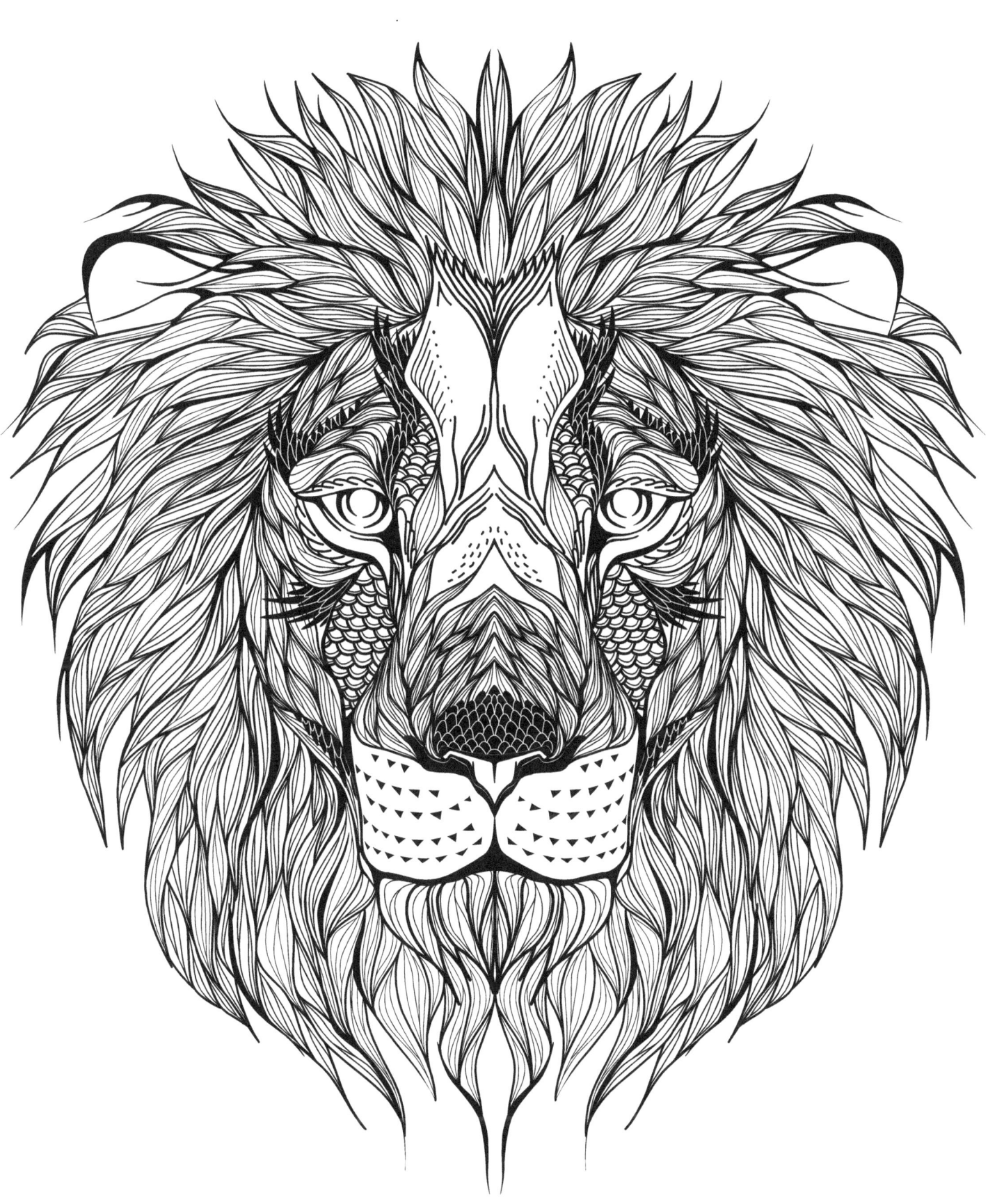

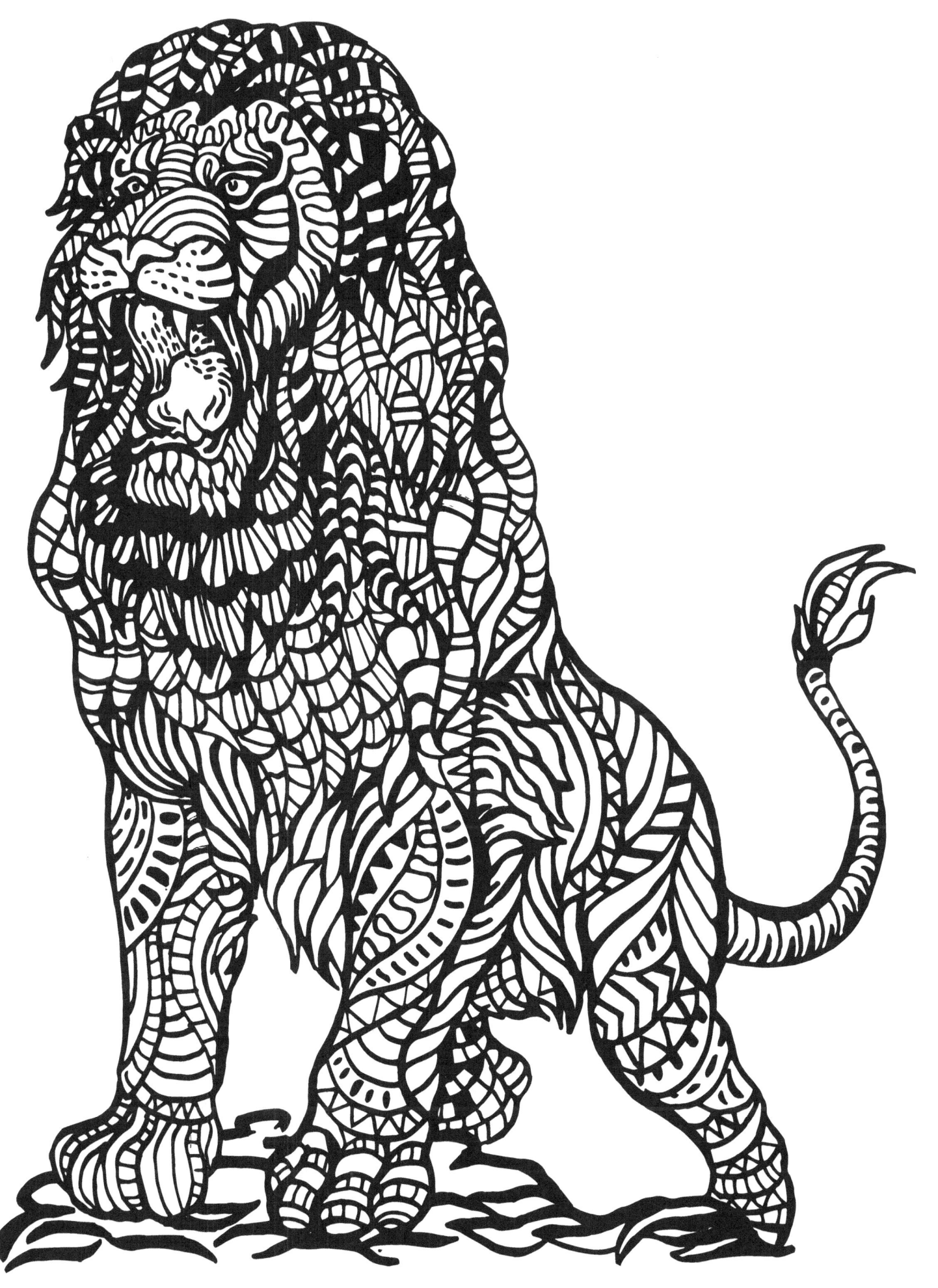

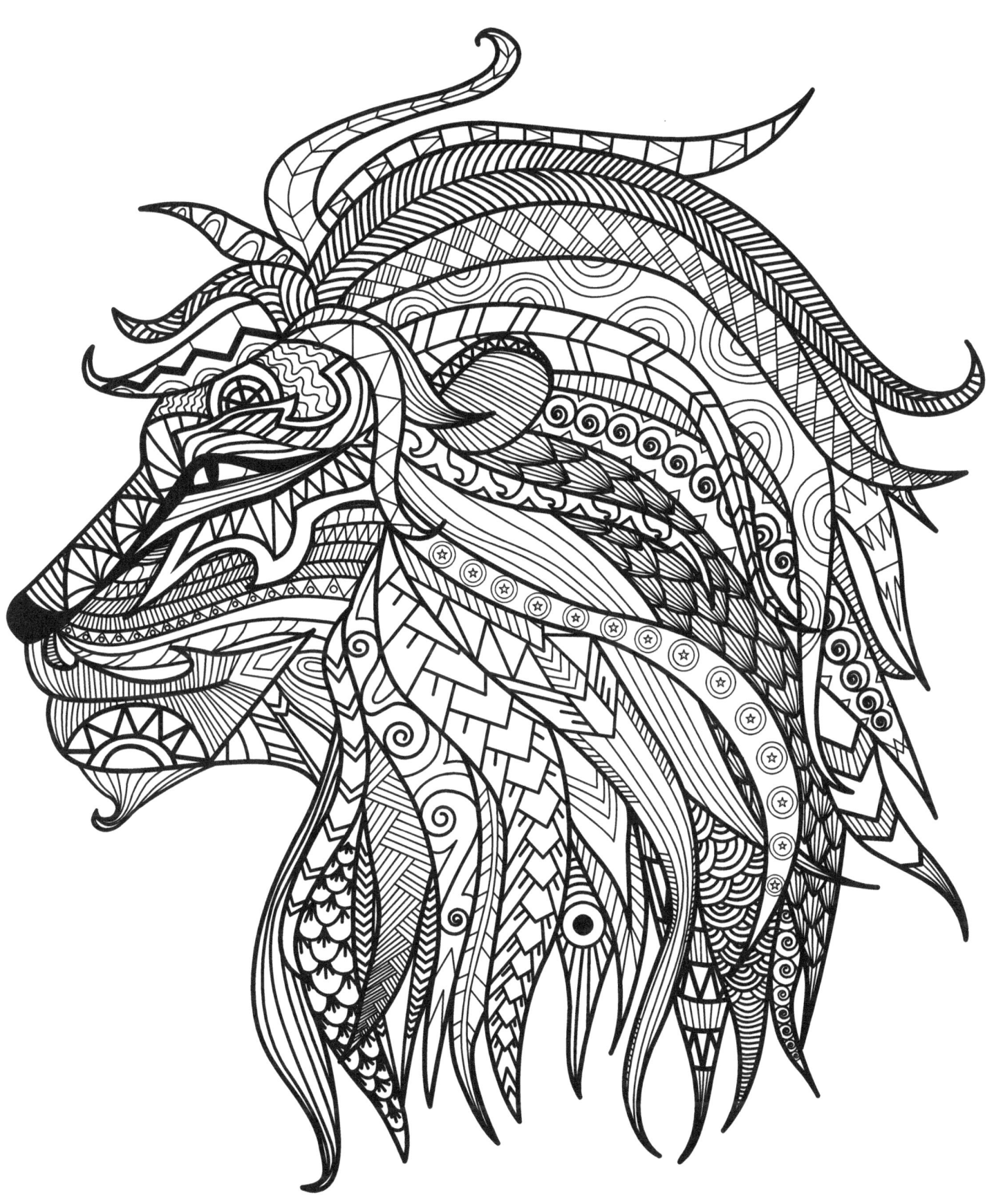

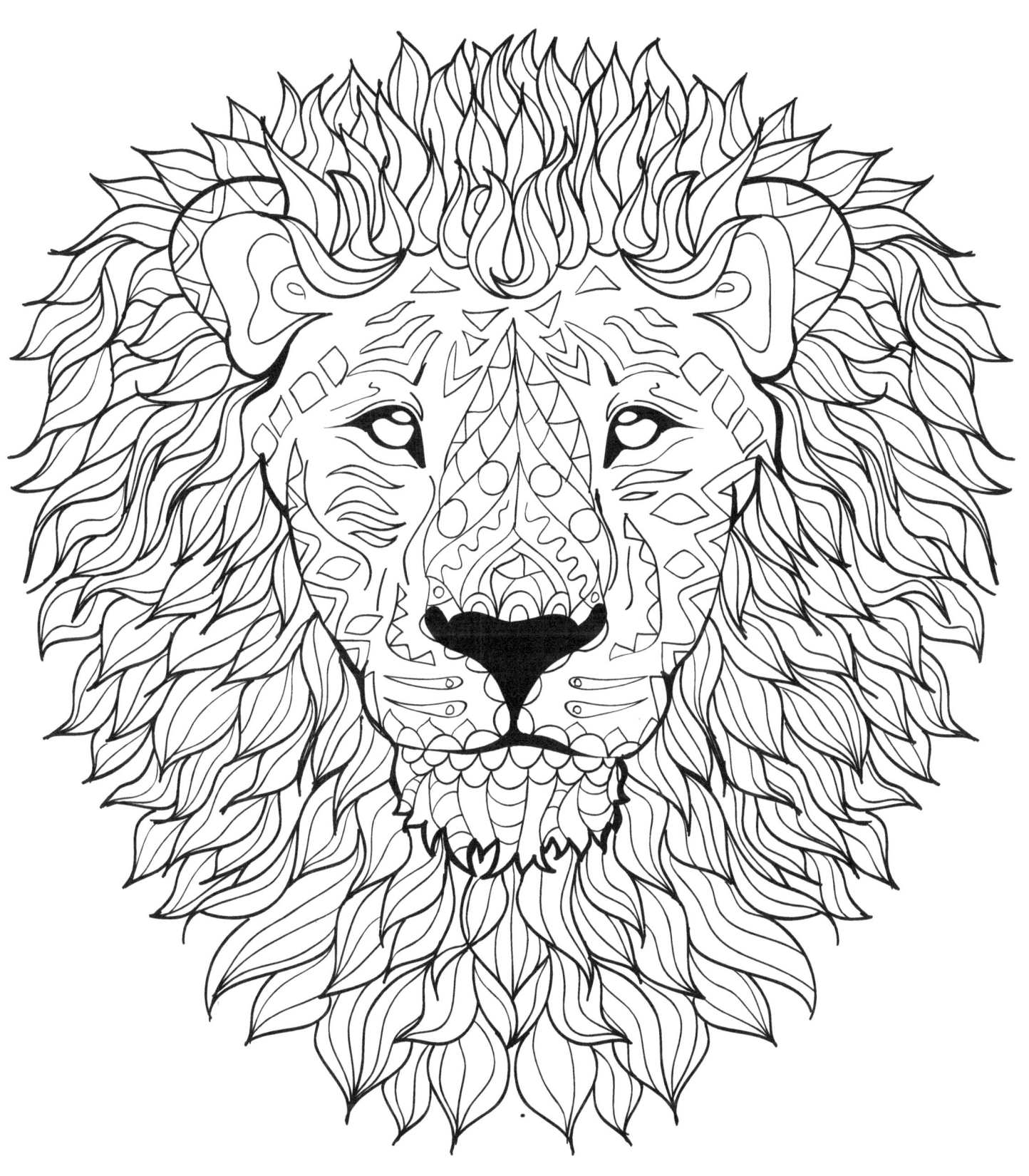

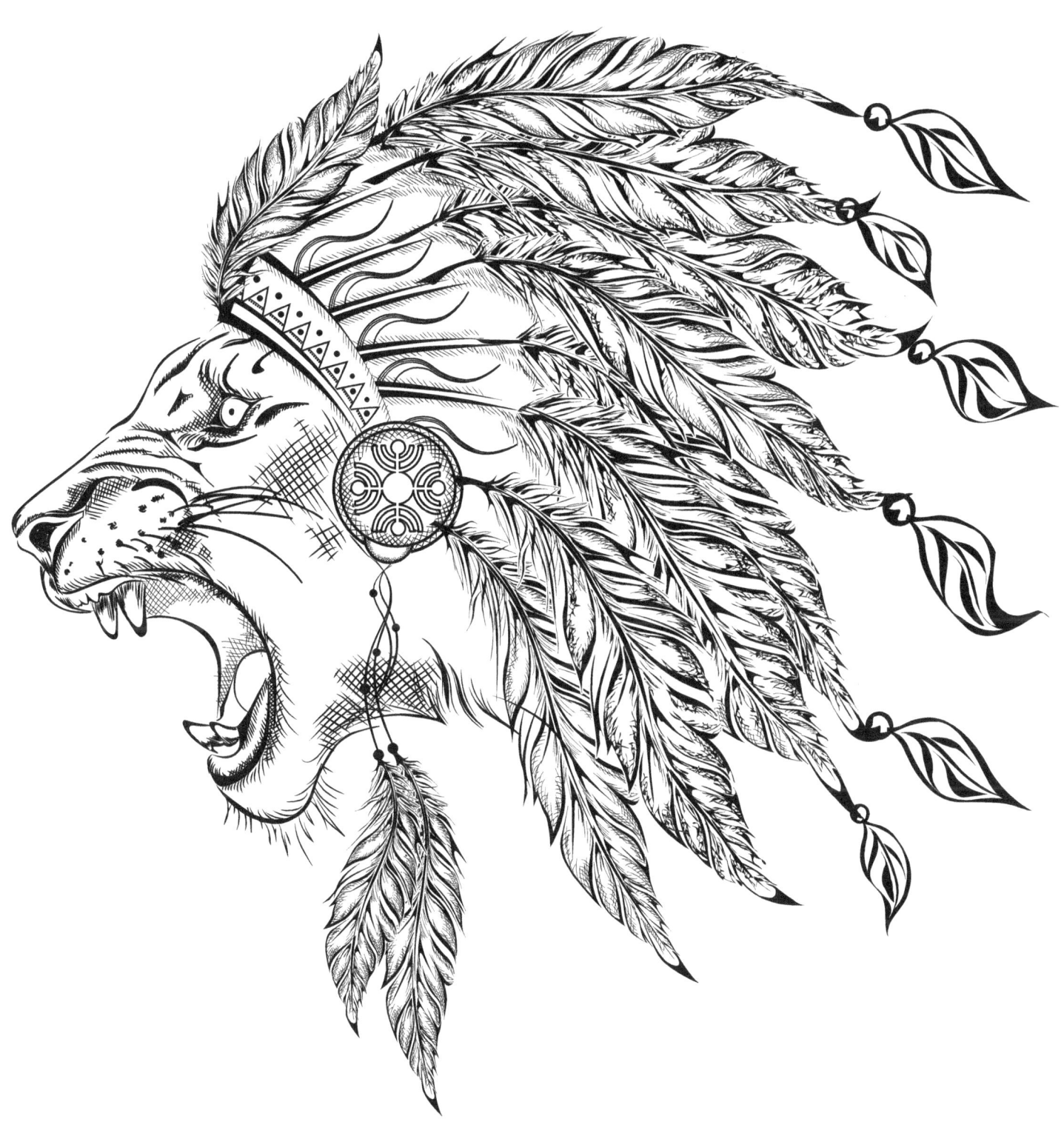

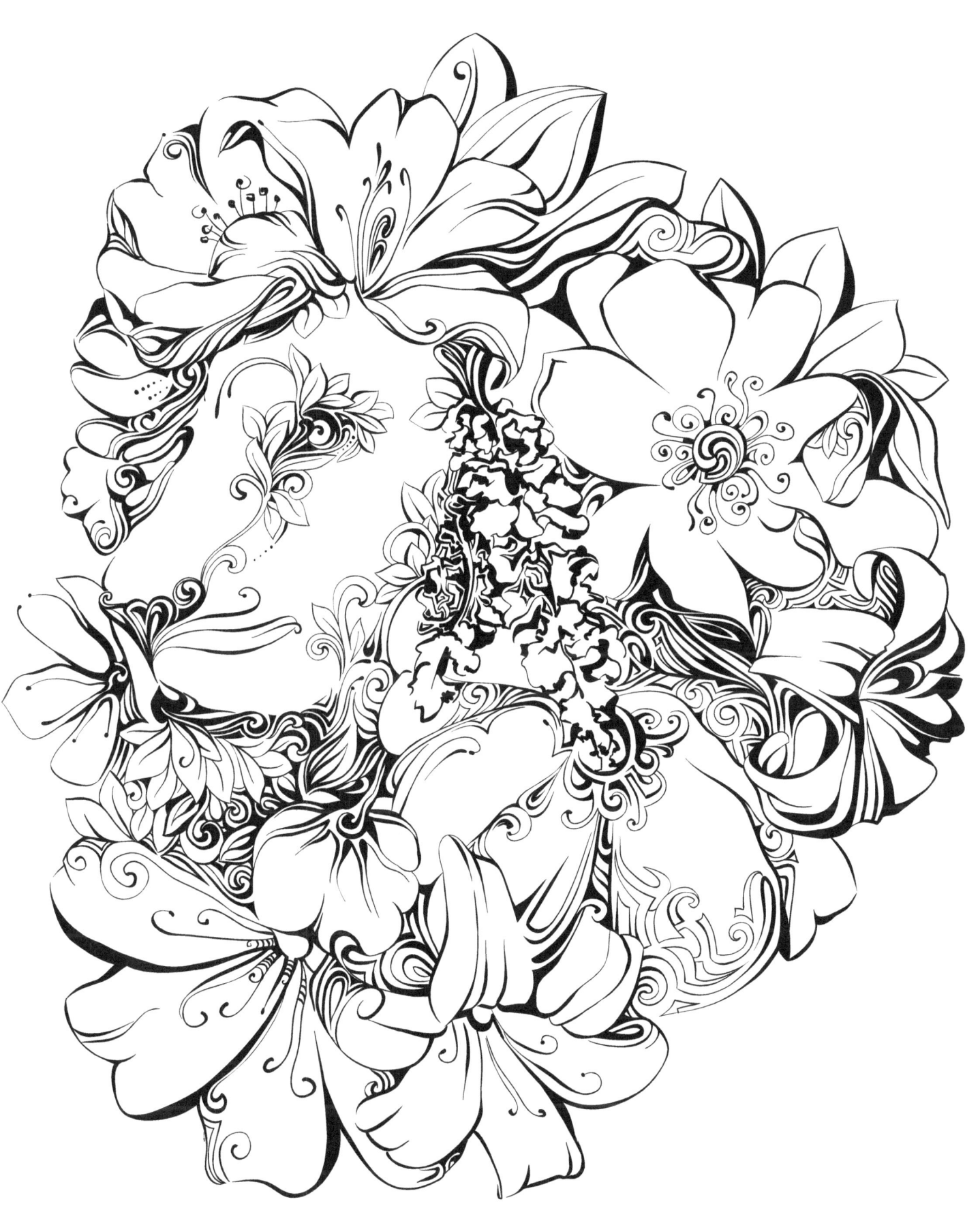

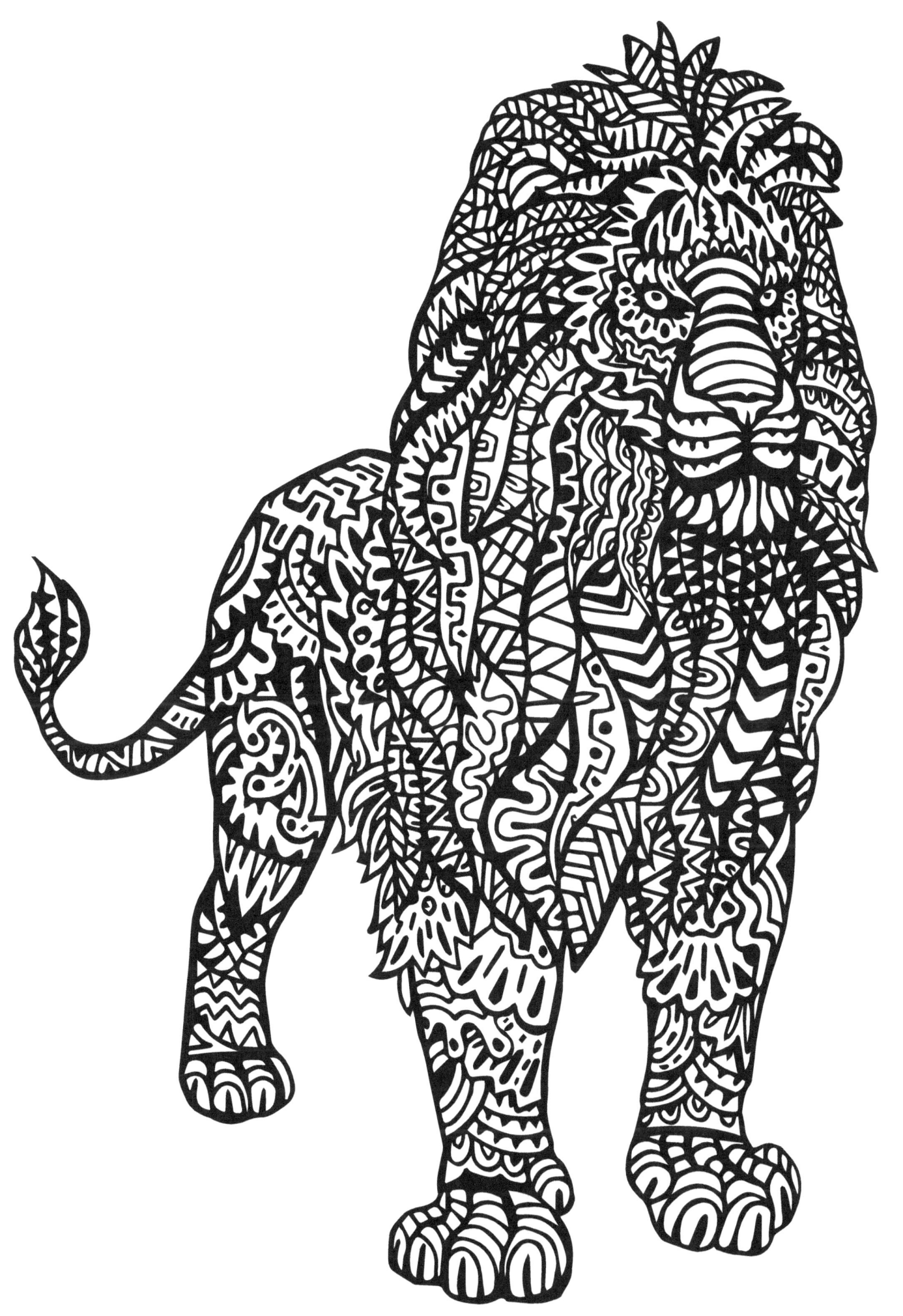

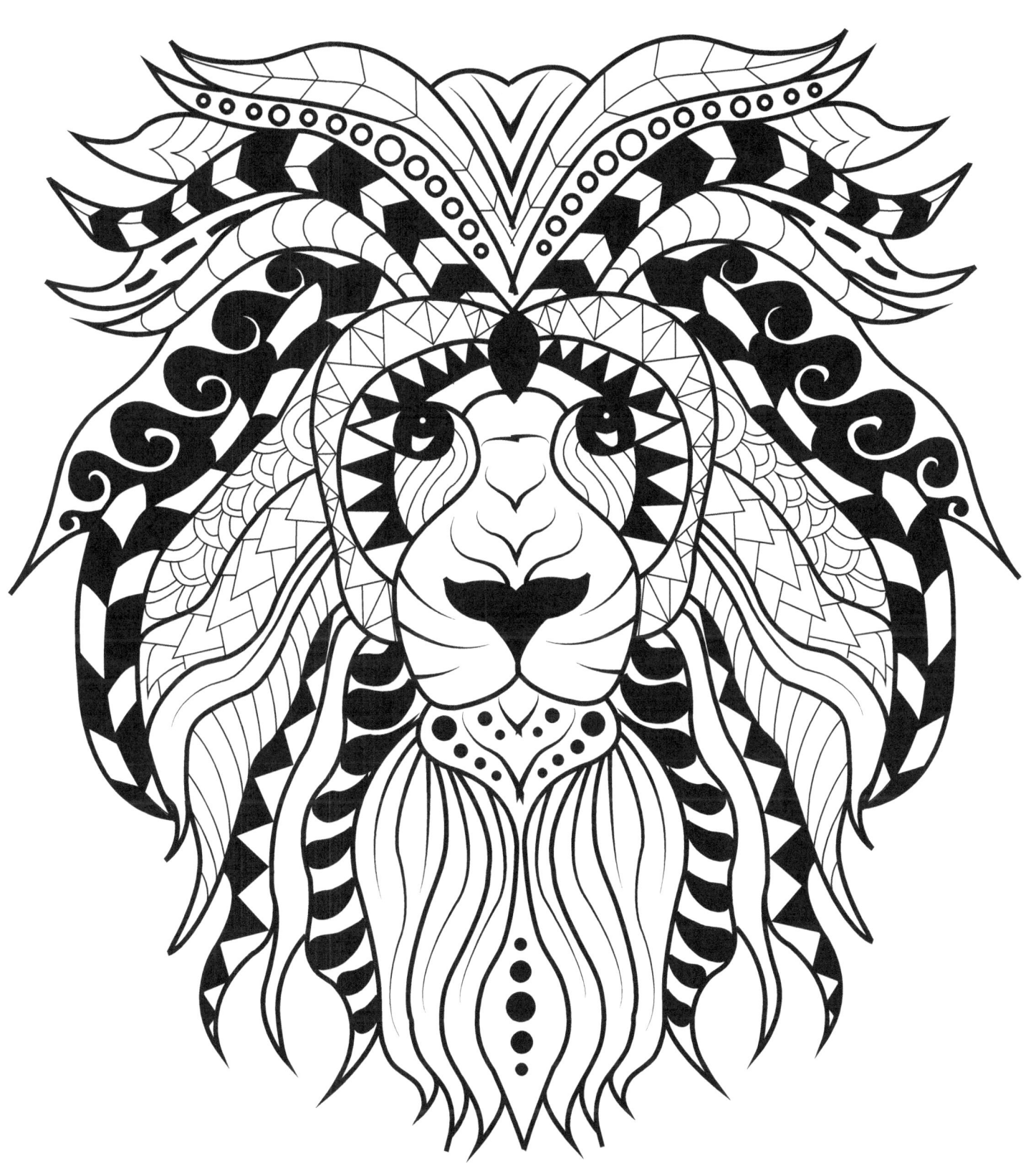

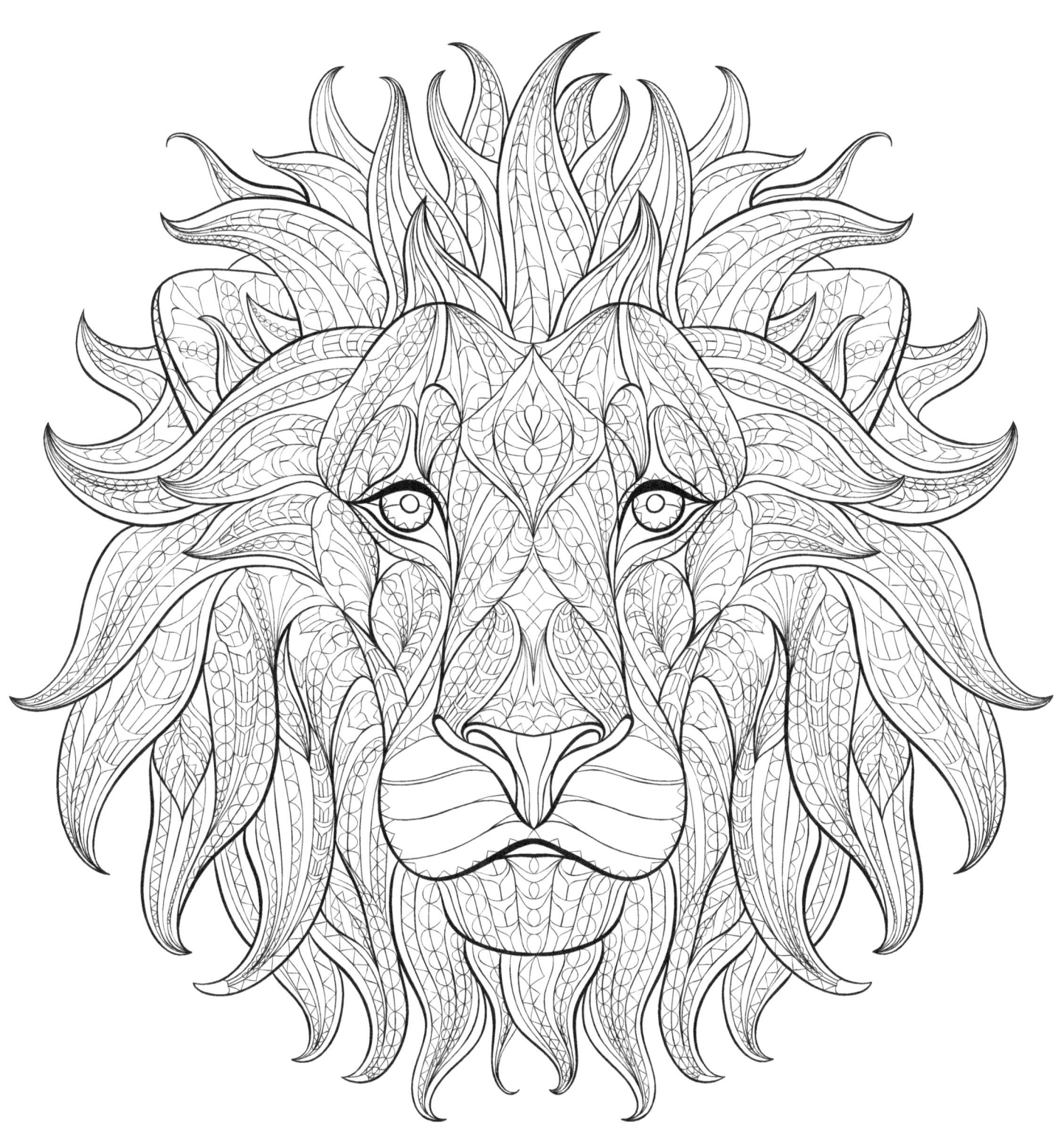

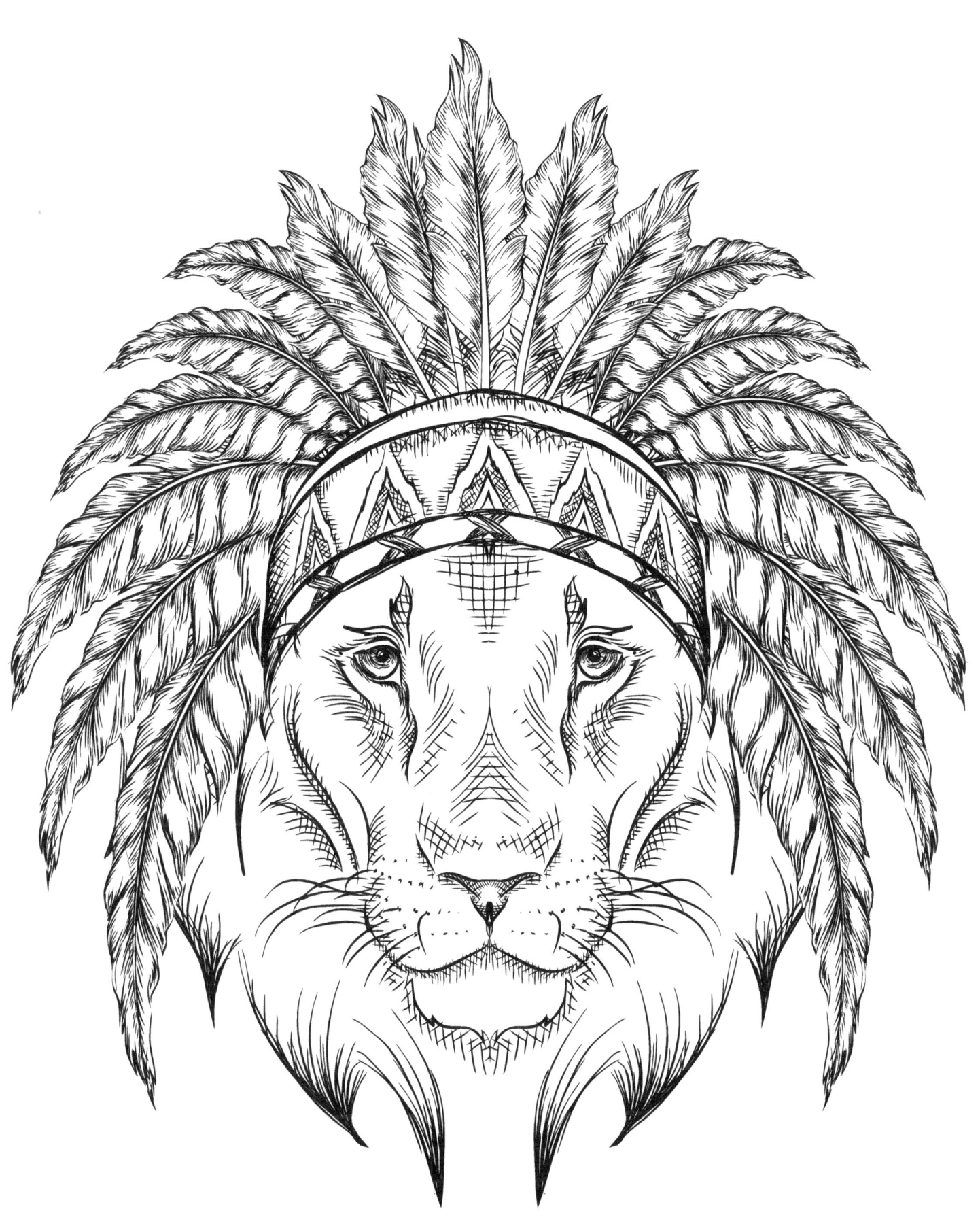

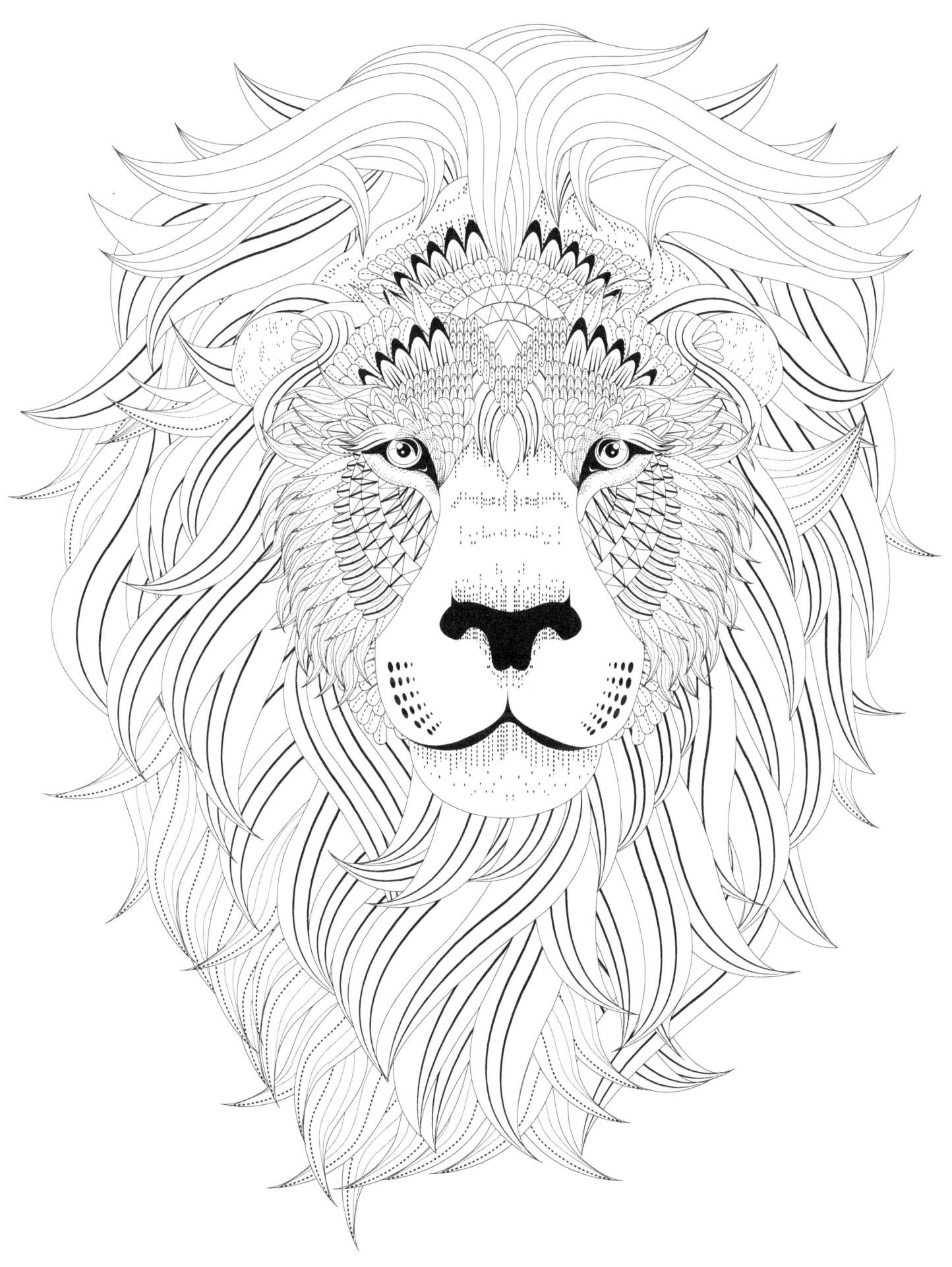

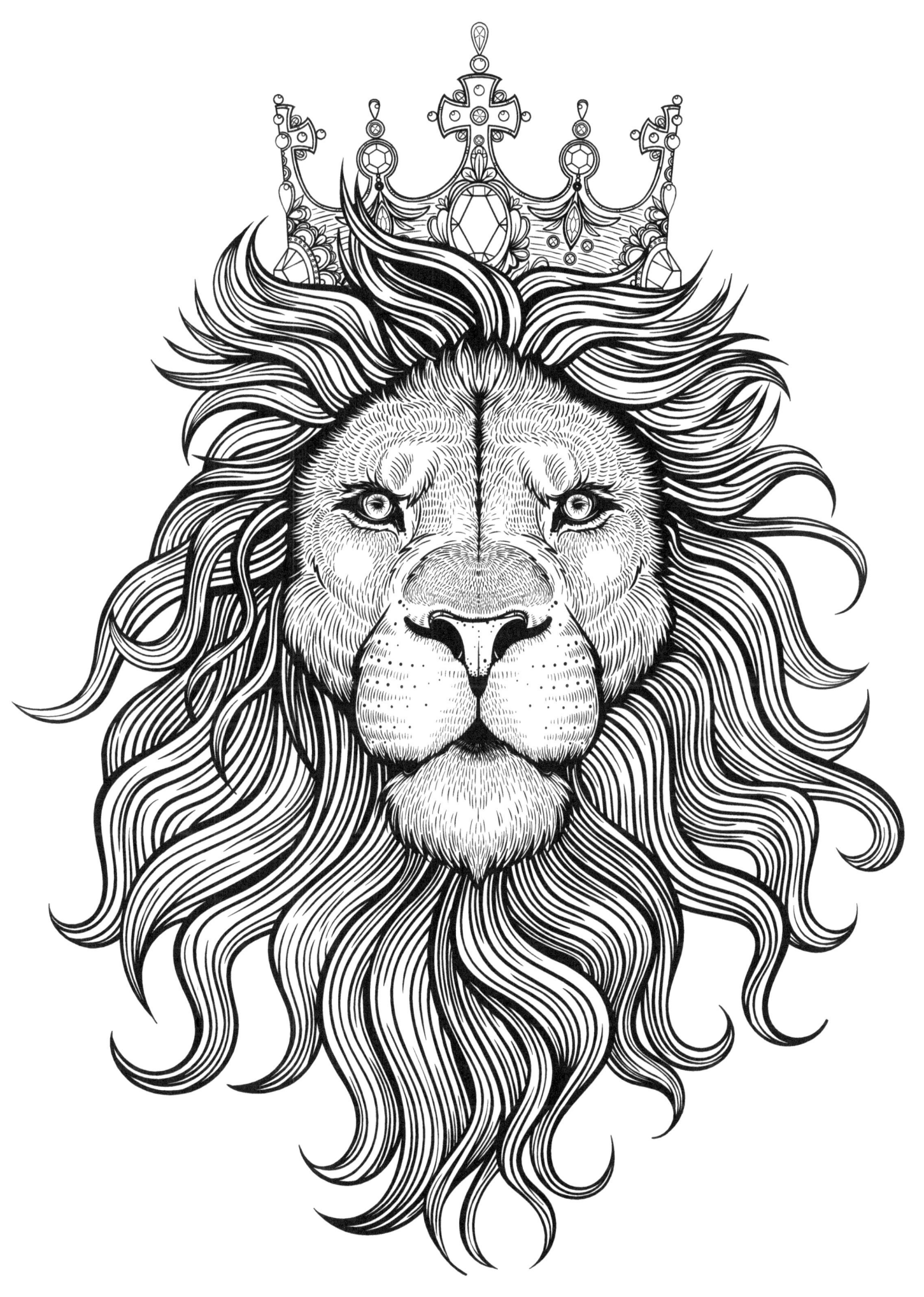

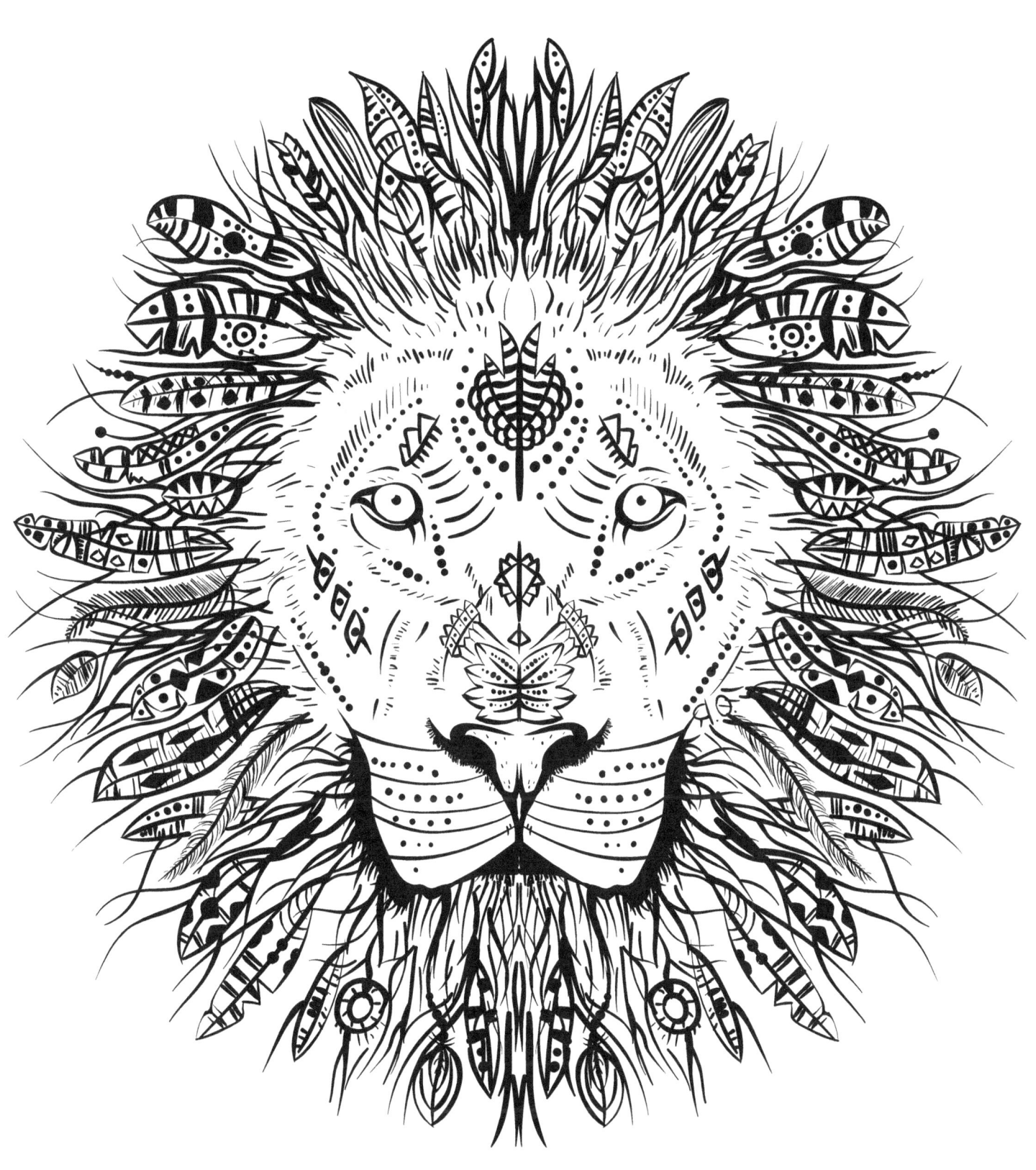

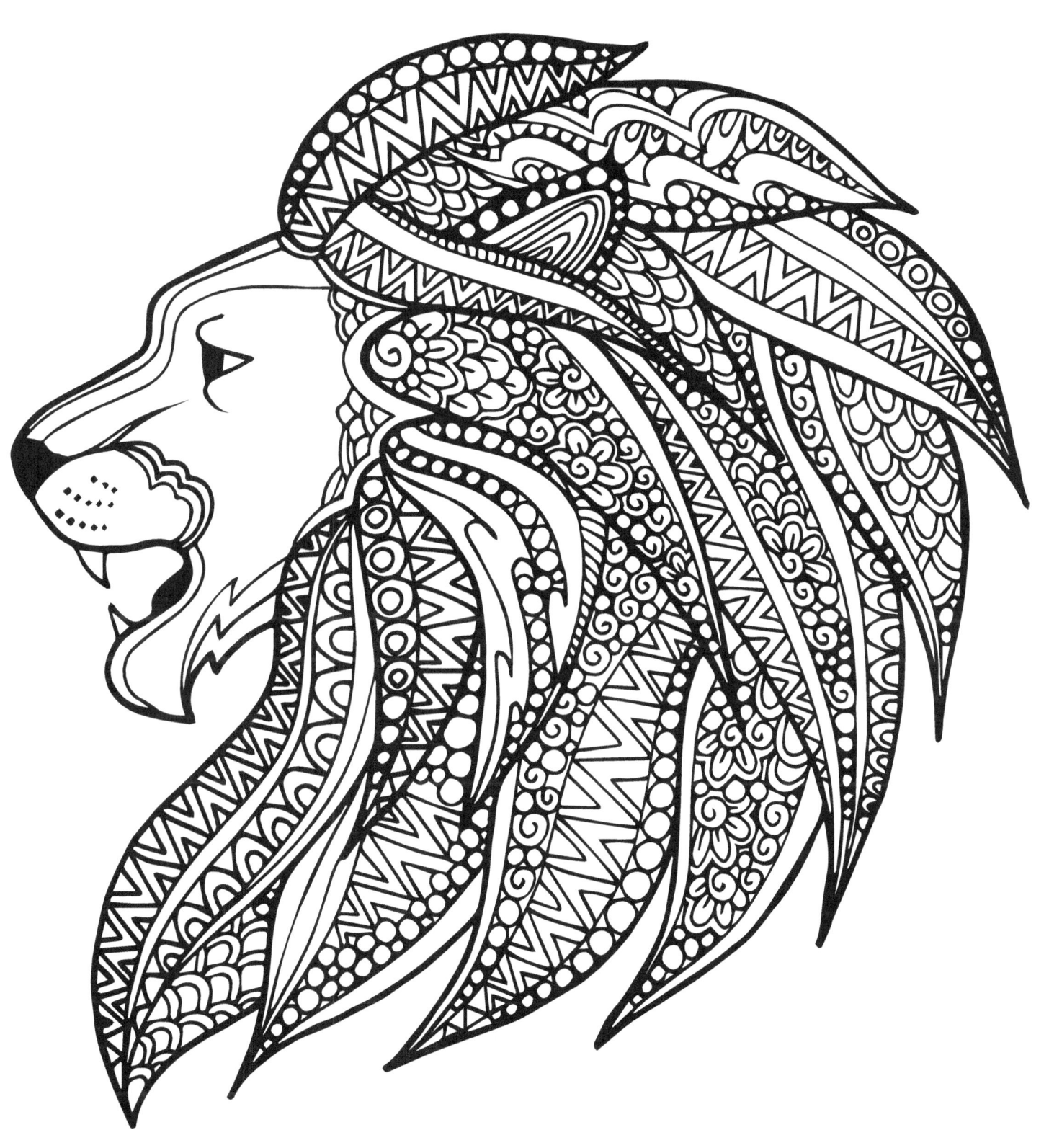

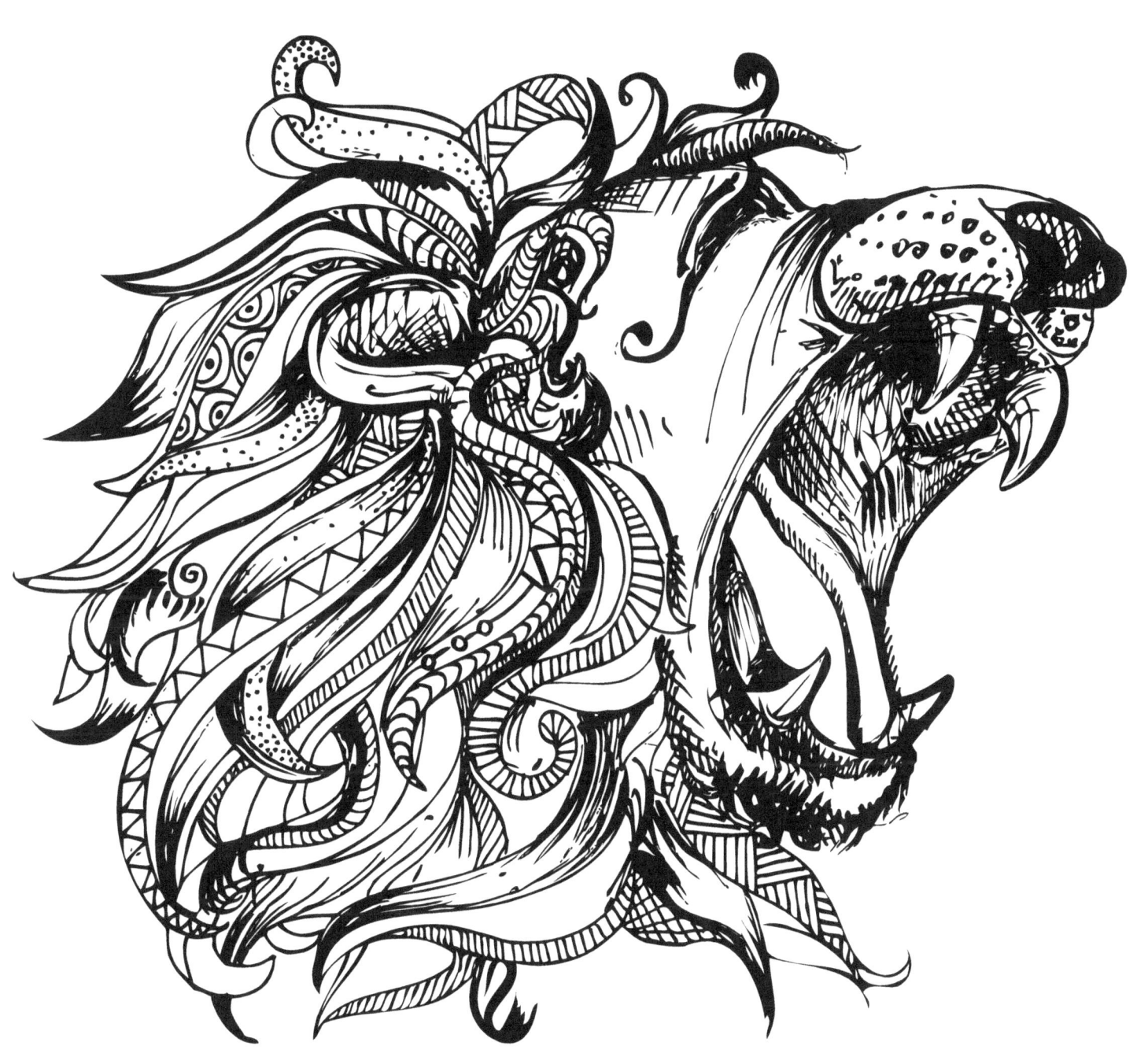

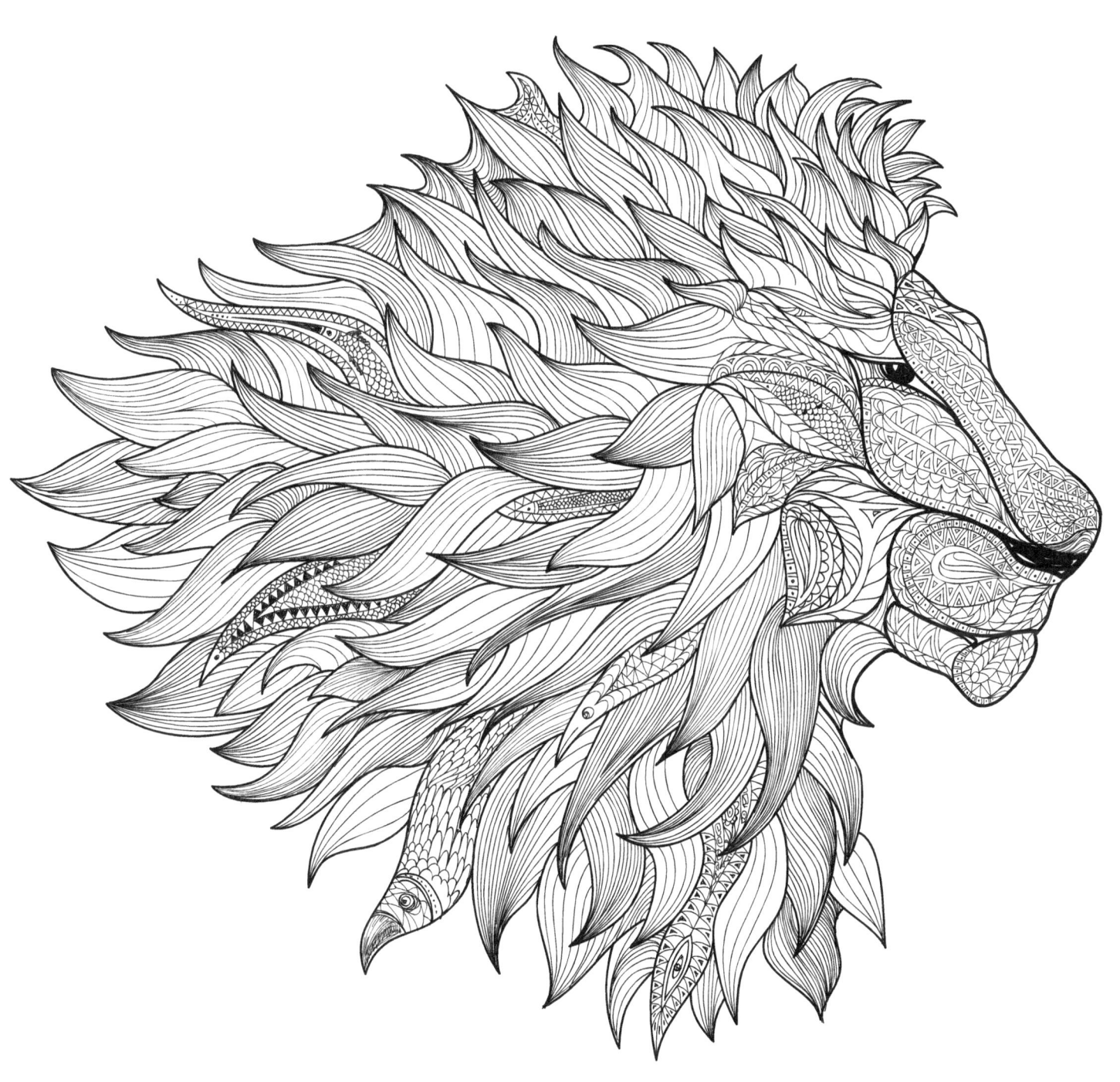

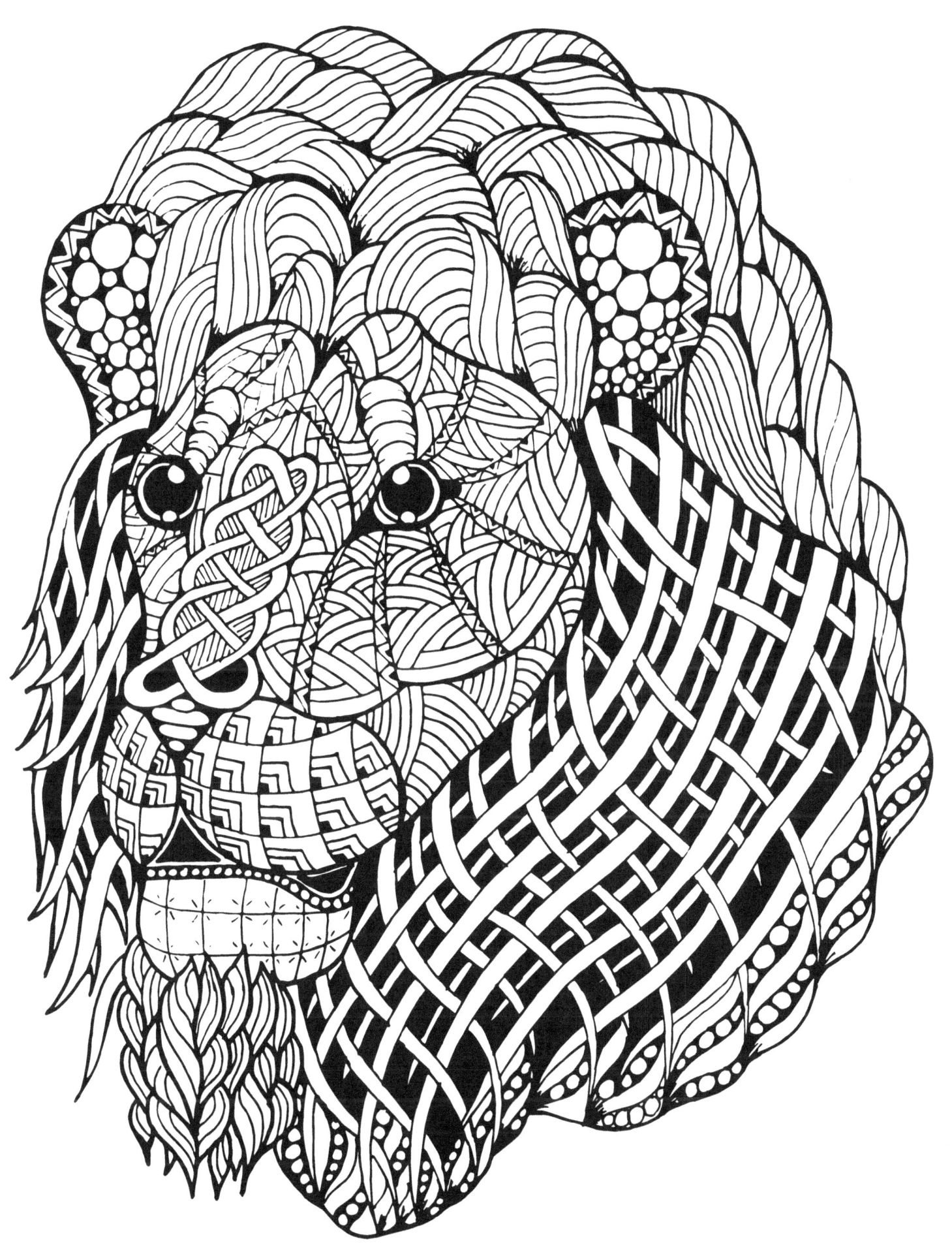

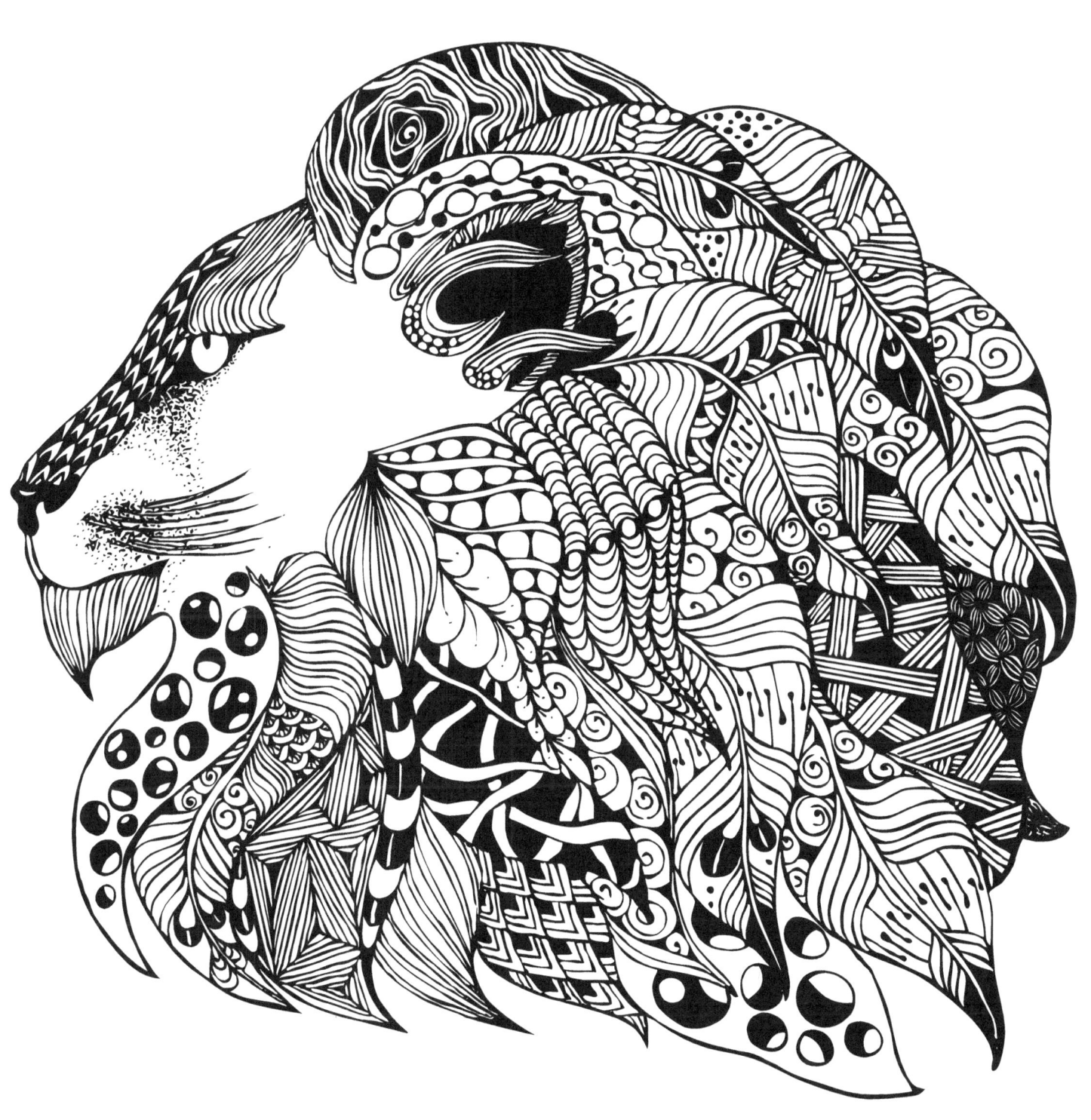

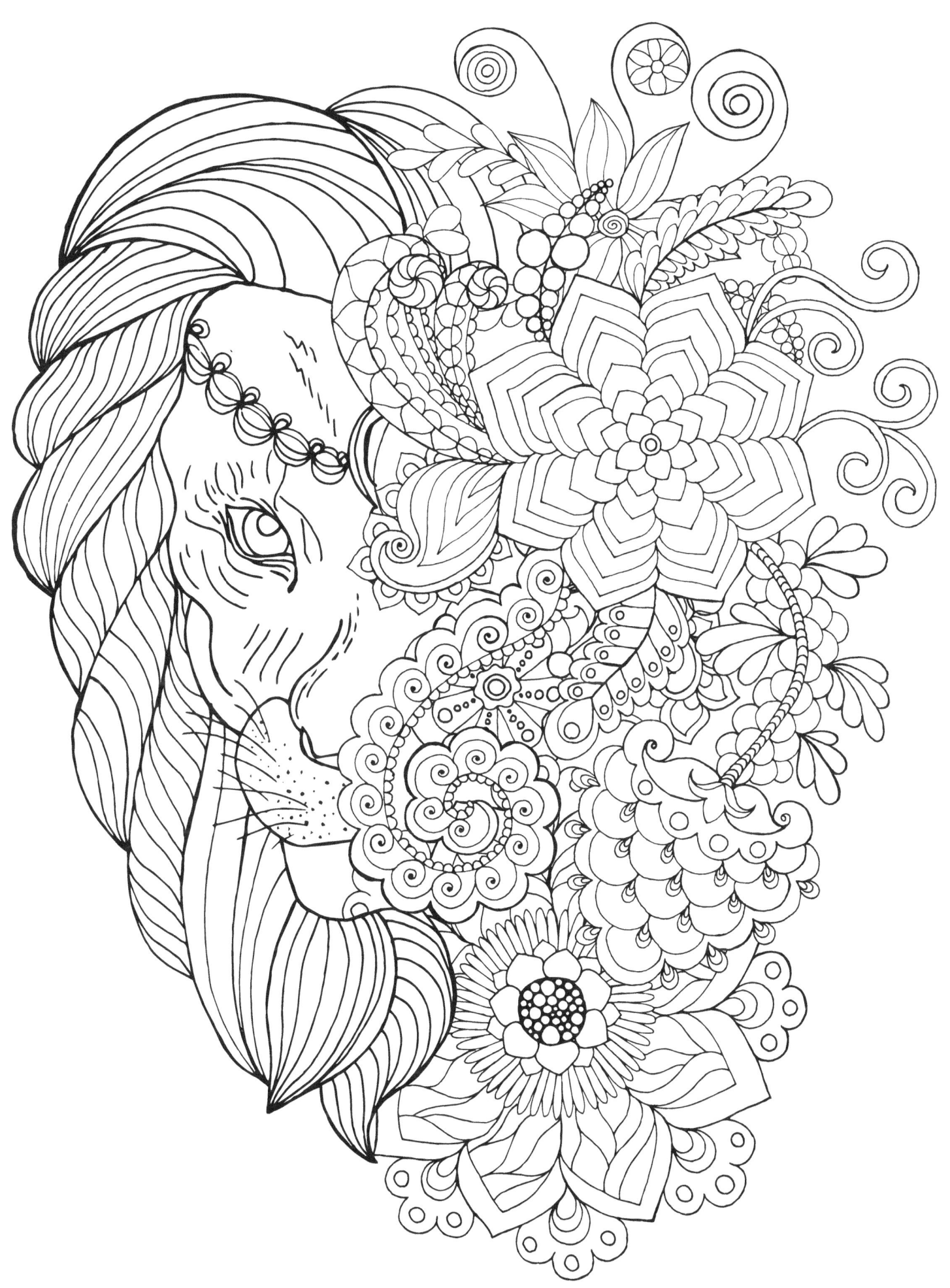

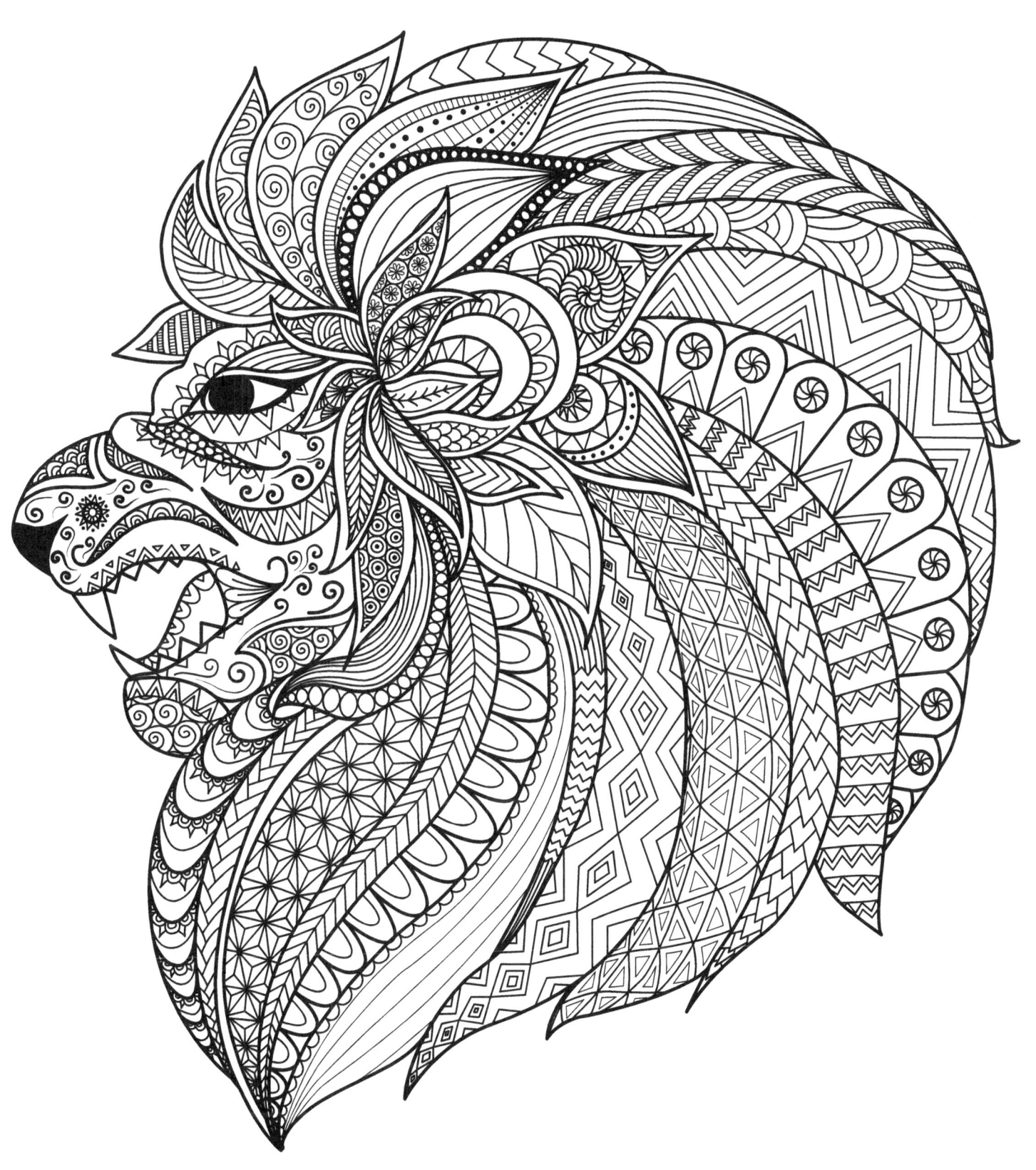

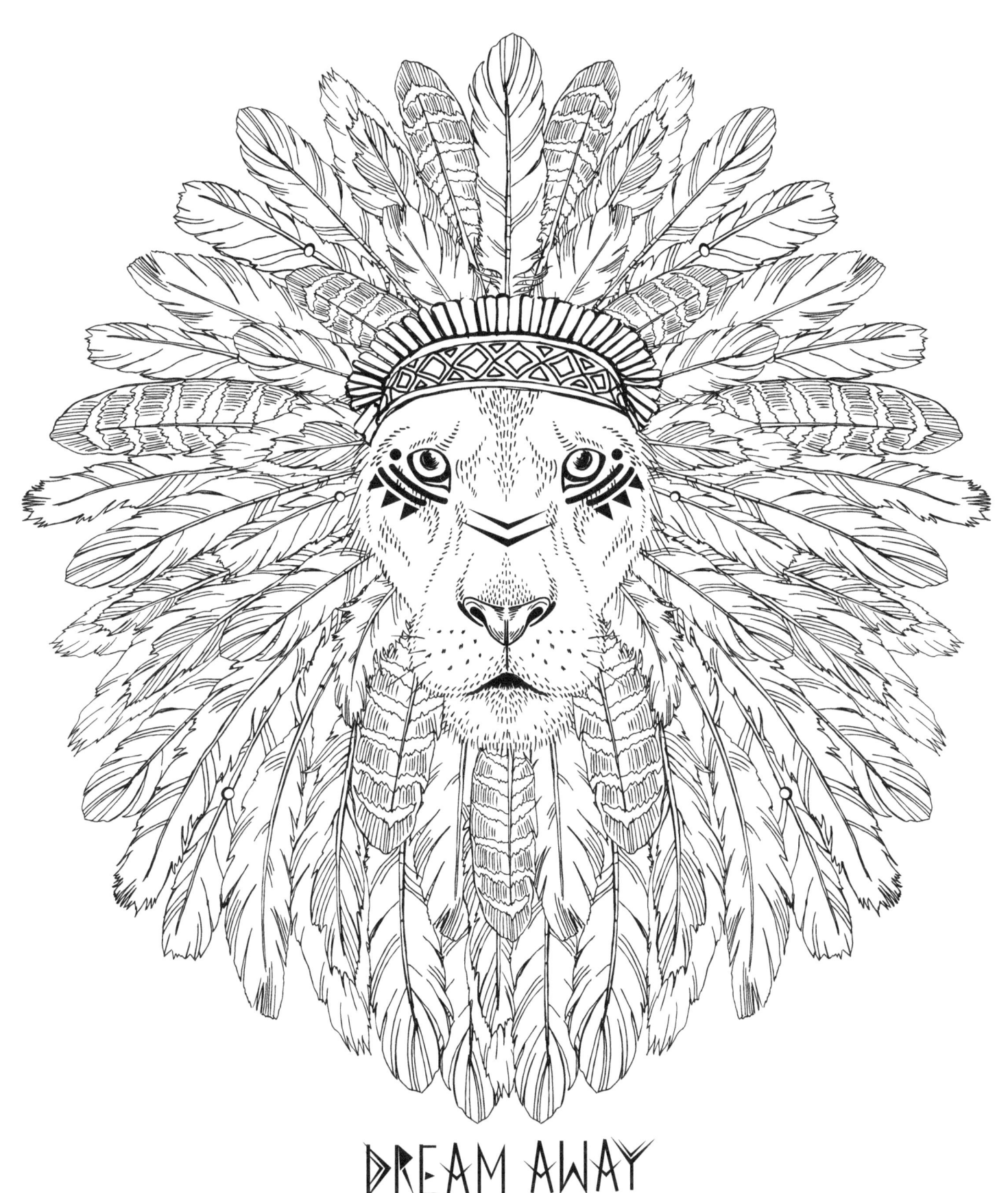

DREAM AWAY

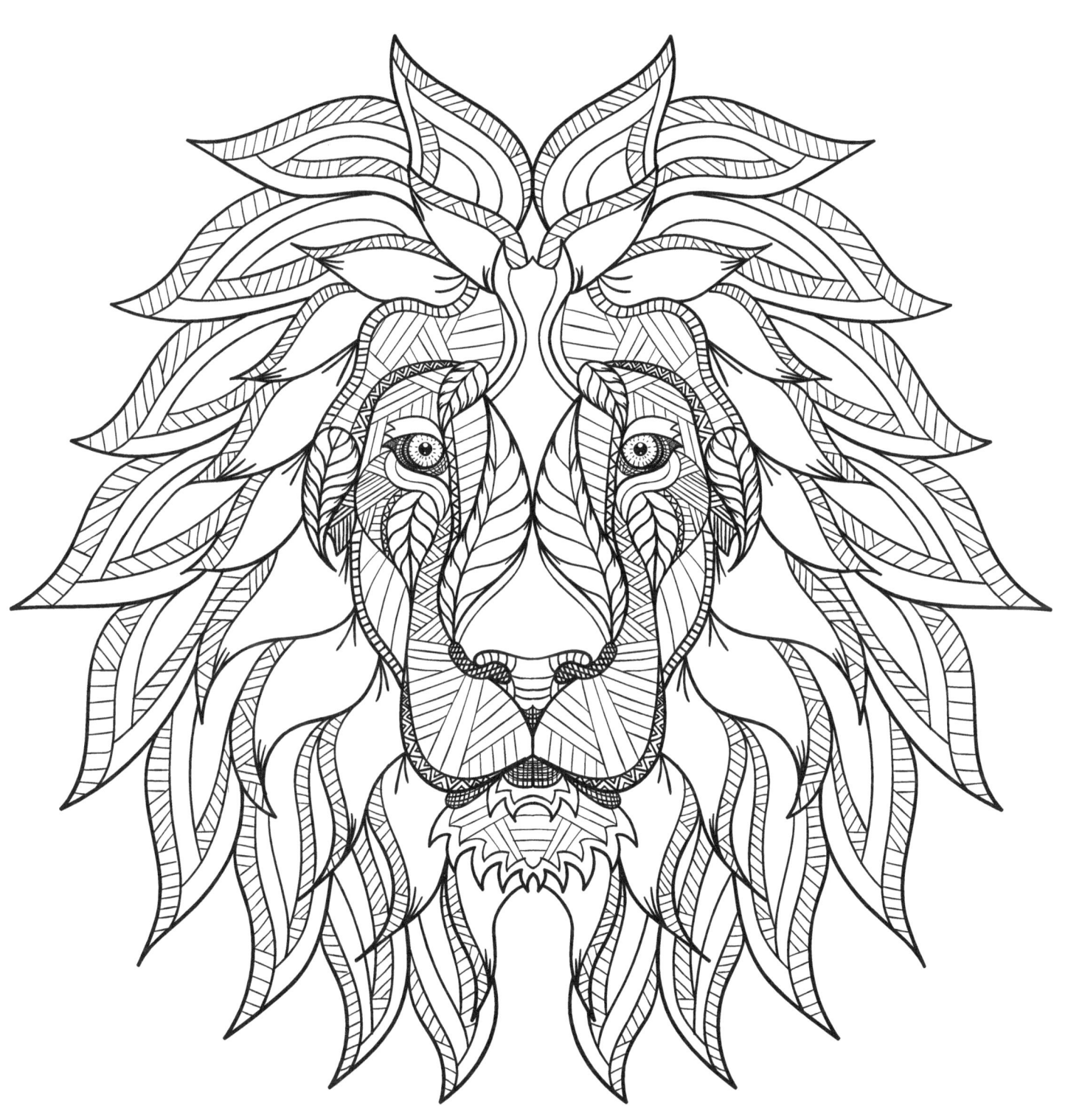

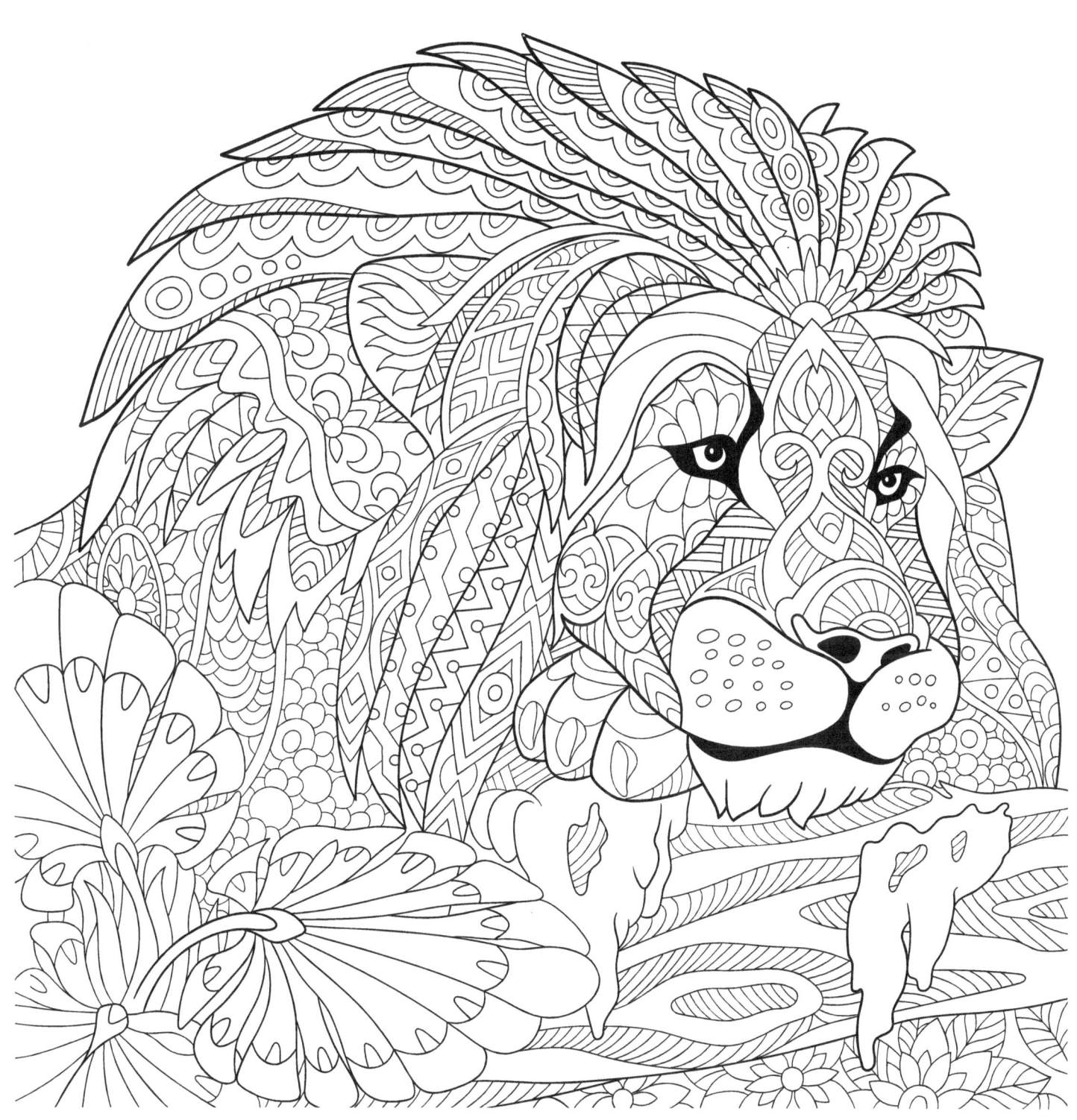

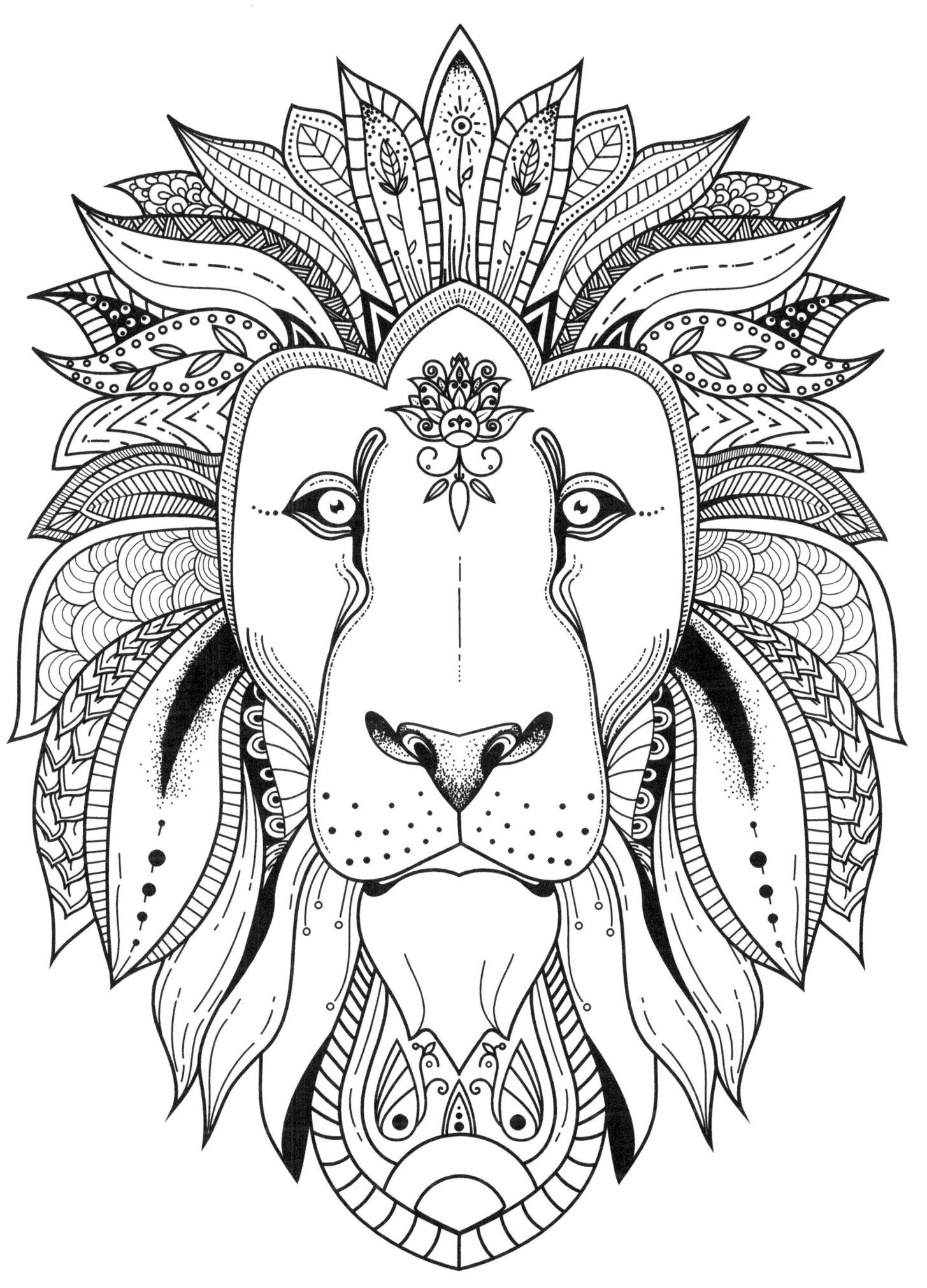

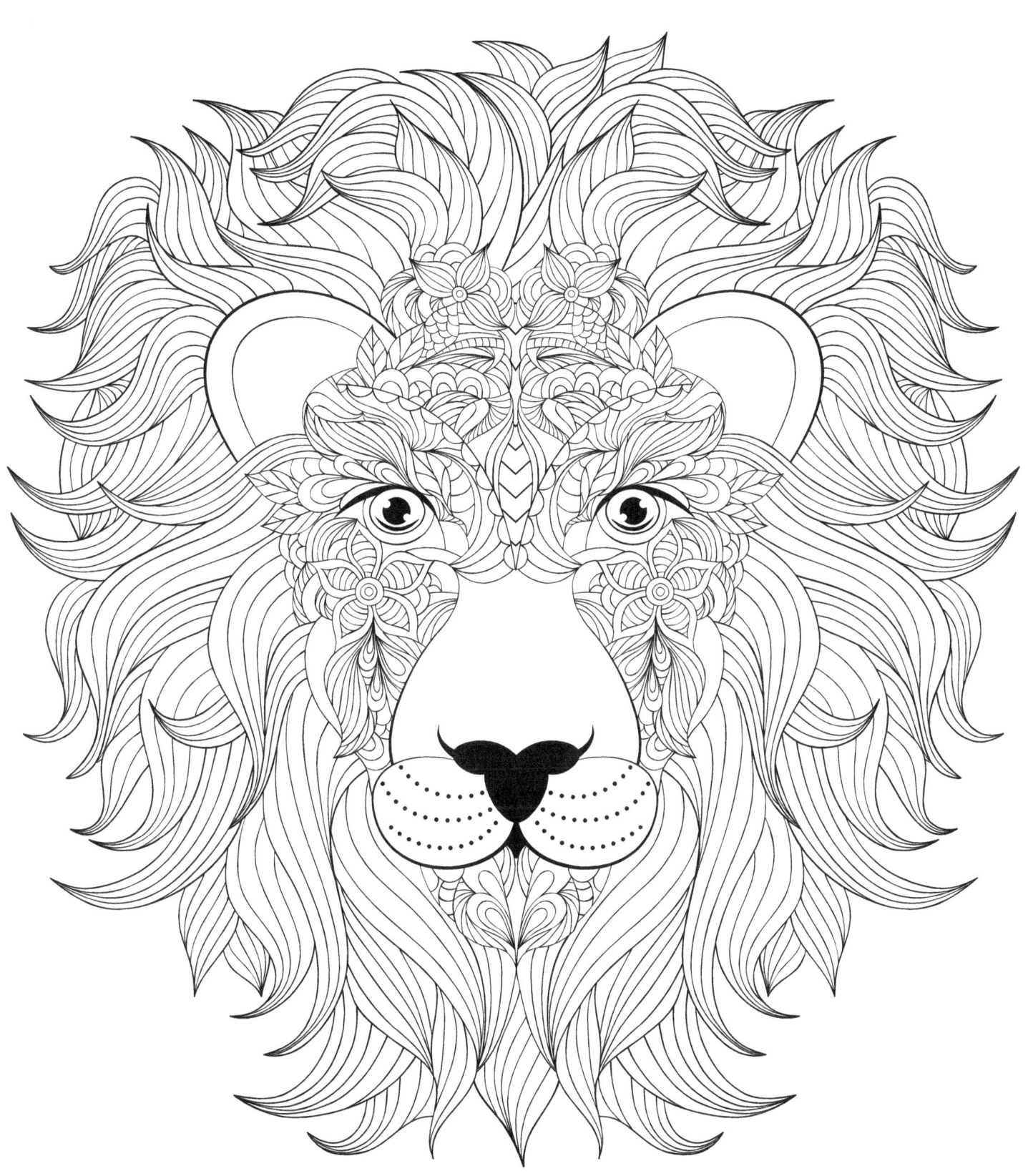

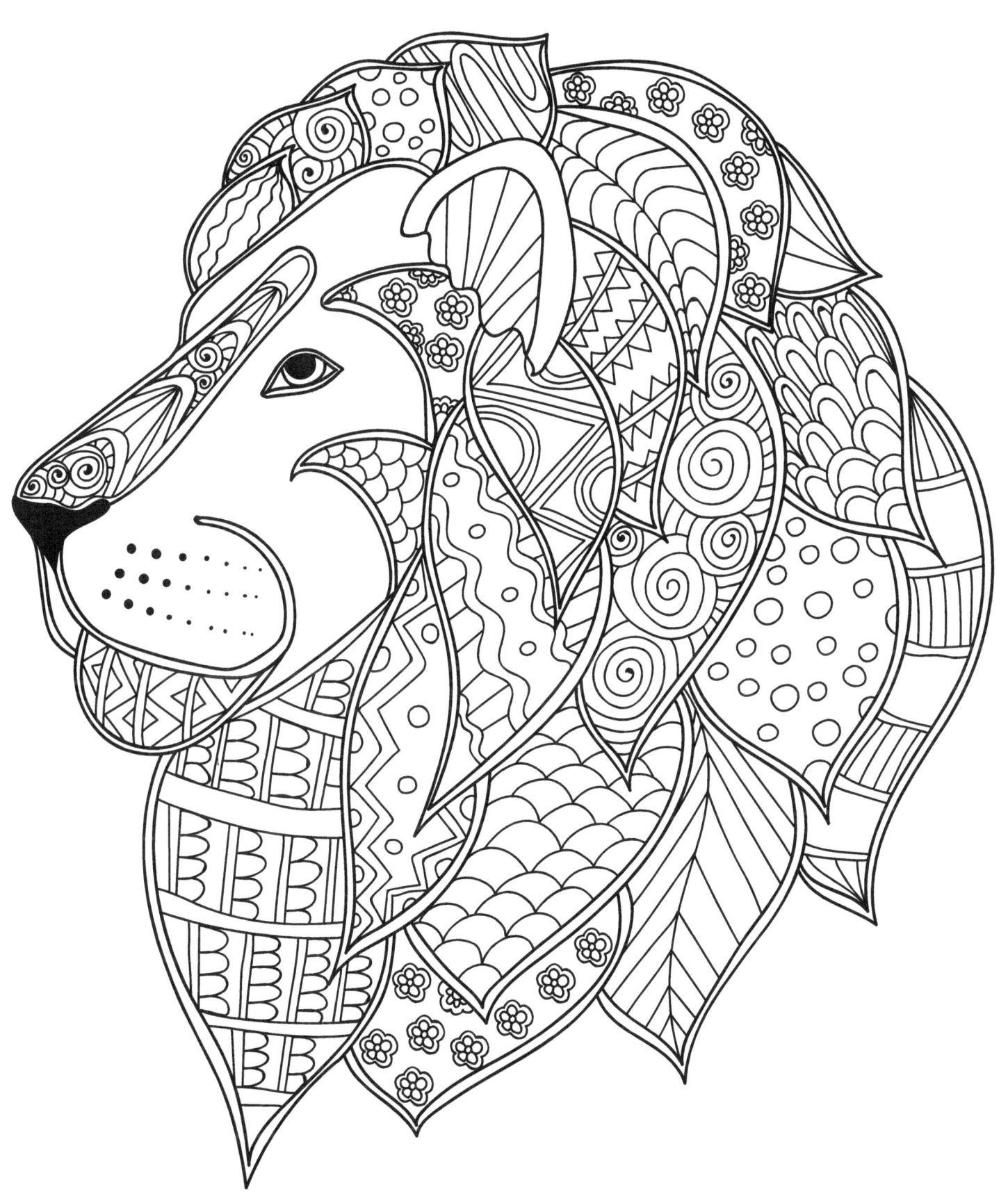

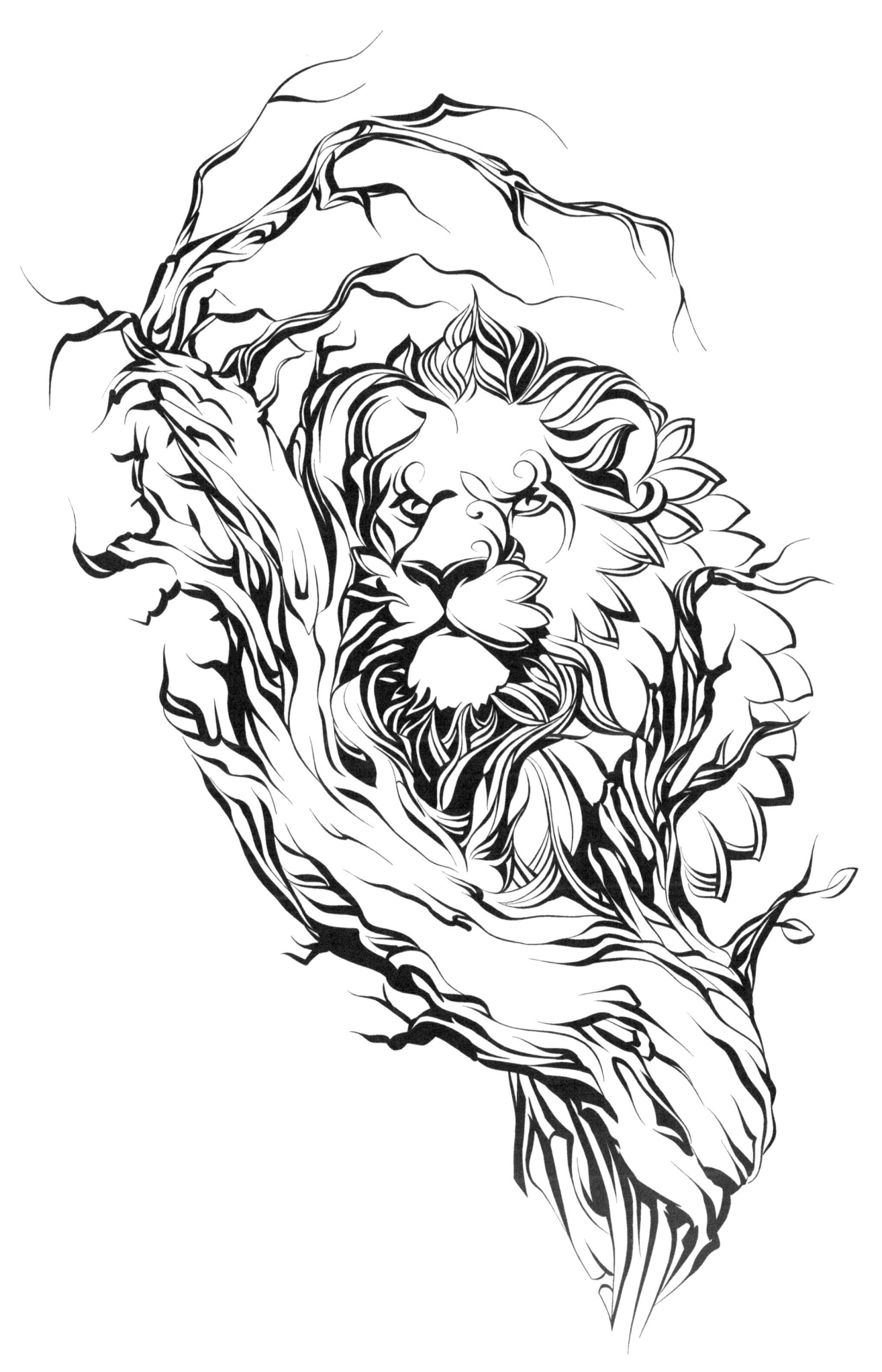

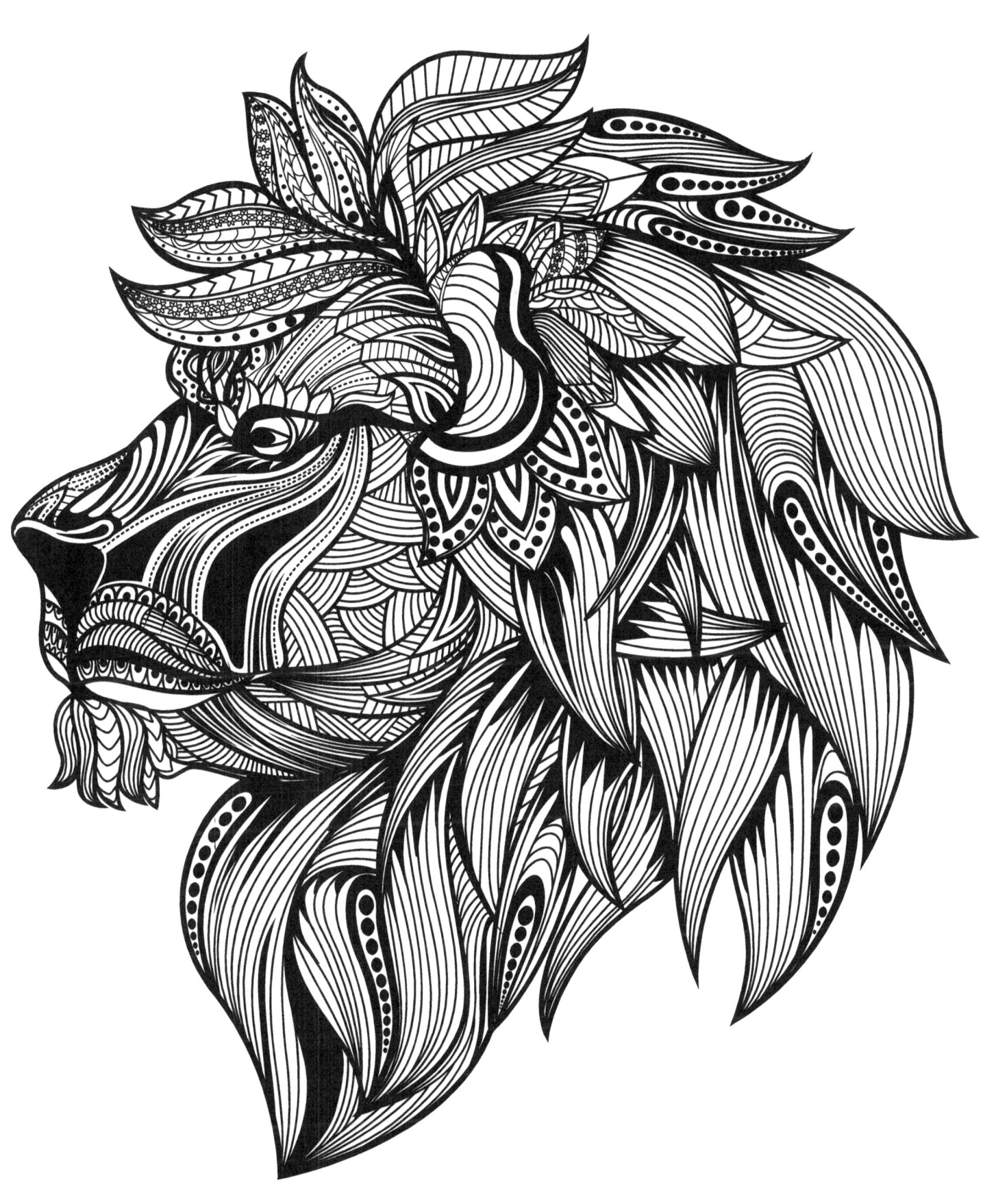

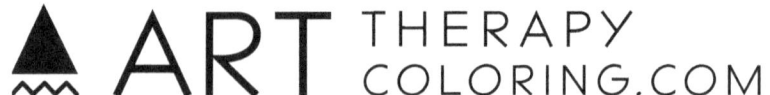

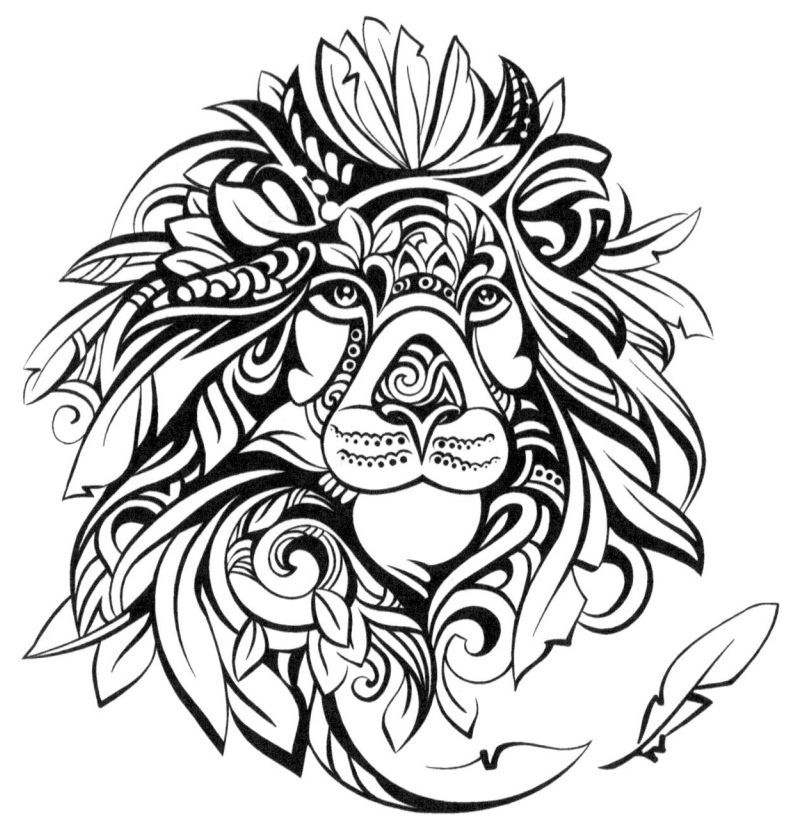

Did You Enjoy Our Coloring Book?

We Want To Hear About It!

Help spread the word about our coloring books! The best way to spread the word is through reviews. We know how busy you are, especially with all of that coloring, but we would appreciate it!

Visit our website at www.arttherapycoloring.com

Over 200 Art Therapy Coloring Books

See our collection of over 200 Art Therapy Coloring Books for Adults, Men, Women, Seniors, Teens, Kids, Boys, and Girls.

Coloring Books For Adults

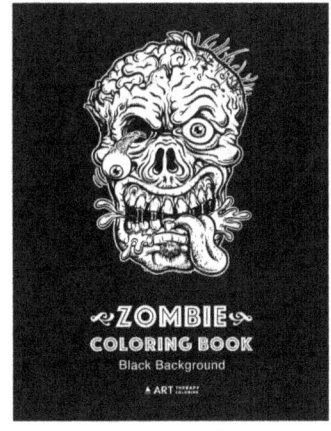

ZOMBIE
COLORING BOOK
Black Background

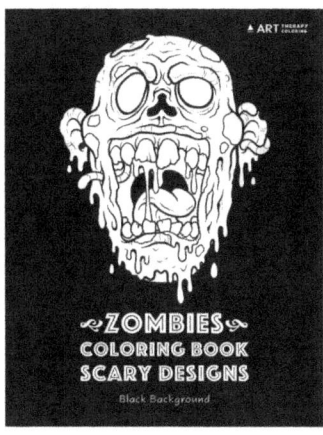

ZOMBIES
COLORING BOOK
SCARY DESIGNS
Black Background

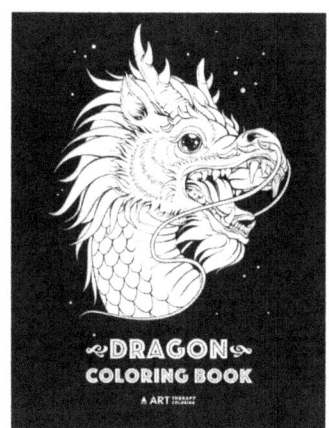

DRAGON
COLORING BOOK

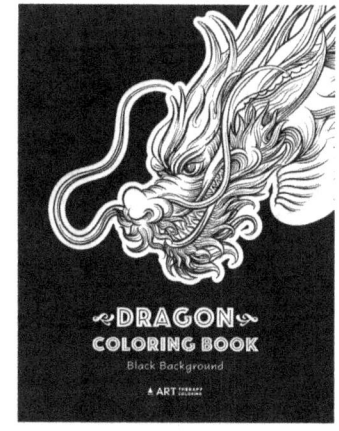

DRAGON
COLORING BOOK
Black Background

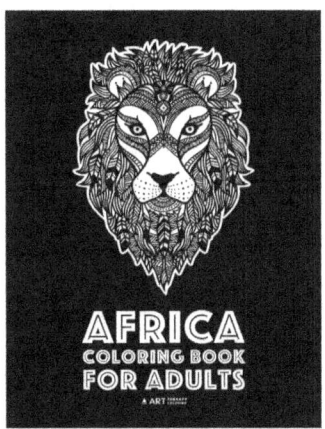

AFRICA
COLORING BOOK
FOR ADULTS

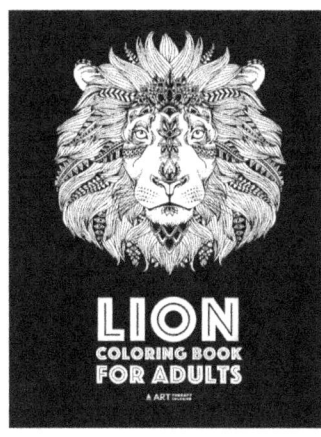

LION
COLORING BOOK
FOR ADULTS

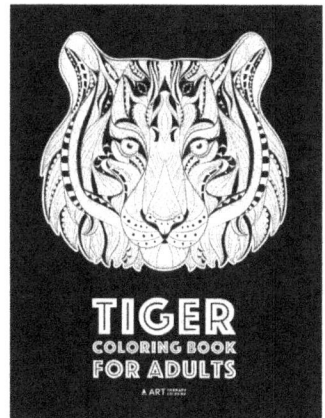

TIGER
COLORING BOOK
FOR ADULTS

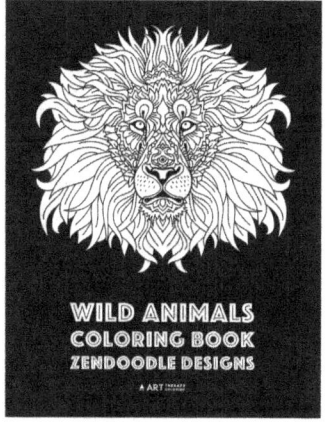

WILD ANIMALS
COLORING BOOK
ZENDOODLE DESIGNS

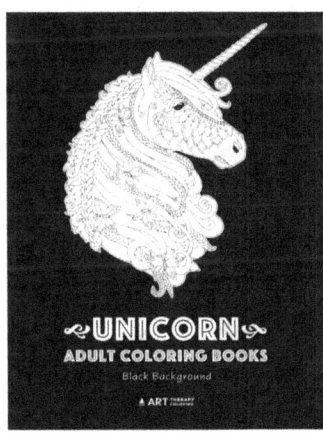

UNICORN
ADULT COLORING BOOKS
Black Background

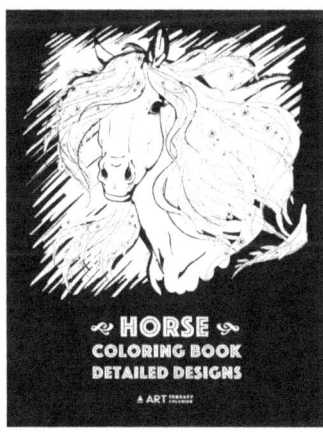

HORSE
COLORING BOOK
DETAILED DESIGNS

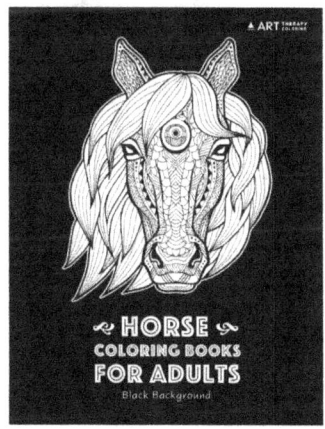

HORSE
COLORING BOOKS
FOR ADULTS
Black Background

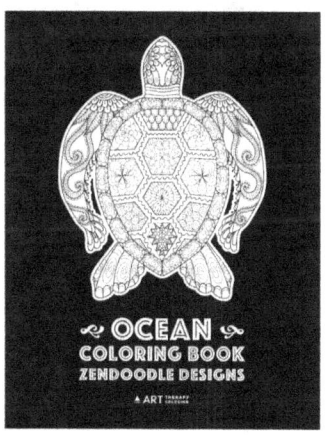

OCEAN
COLORING BOOK
ZENDOODLE DESIGNS

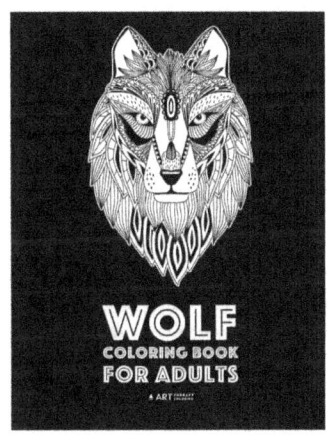

WOLF
COLORING BOOK
FOR ADULTS

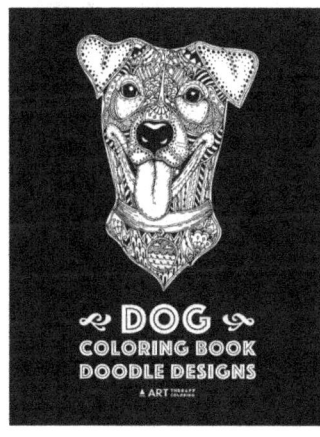

DOG
COLORING BOOK
DOODLE DESIGNS

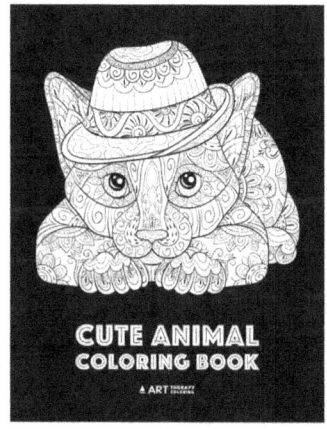

CUTE ANIMAL
COLORING BOOK

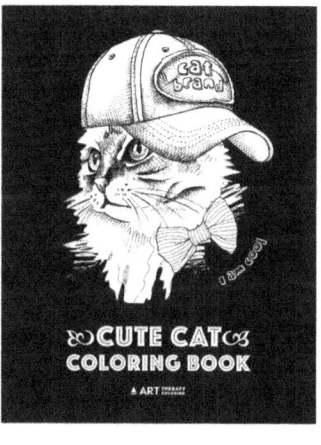

CUTE CAT
COLORING BOOK

Coloring Books For Adults

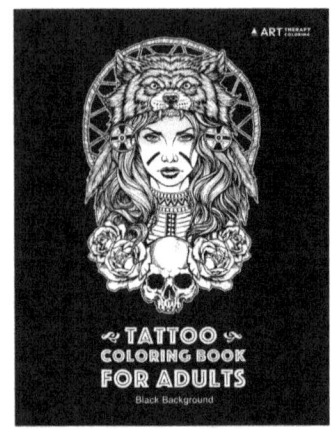

TATTOO
COLORING BOOK
FOR ADULTS
Black Background

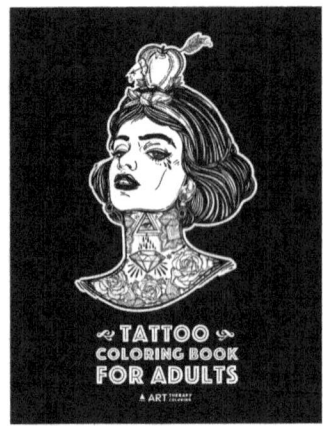

TATTOO
COLORING BOOK
FOR ADULTS

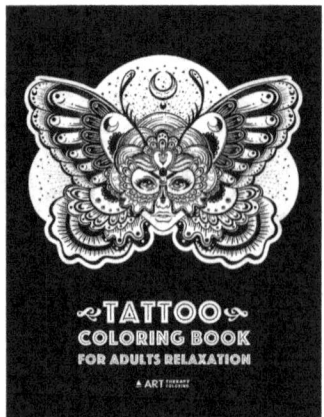

TATTOO
COLORING BOOK
FOR ADULTS RELAXATION

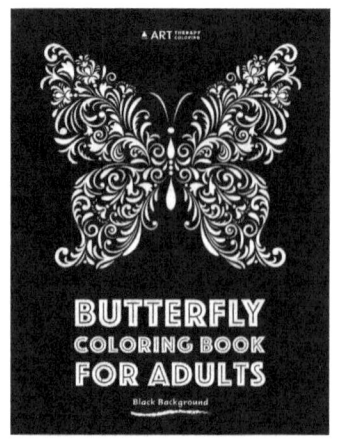

BUTTERFLY
COLORING BOOK
FOR ADULTS
Black Background

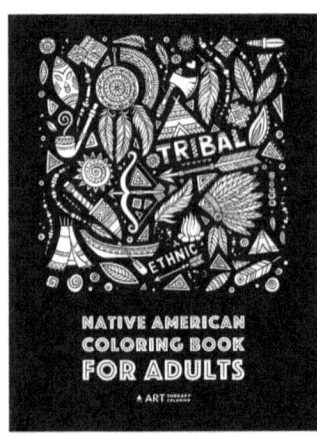

NATIVE AMERICAN
COLORING BOOK
FOR ADULTS

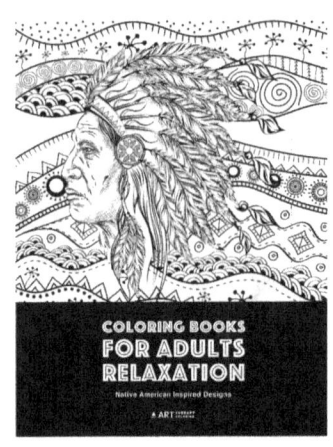

COLORING BOOKS
FOR ADULTS
RELAXATION
Native American Inspired Designs

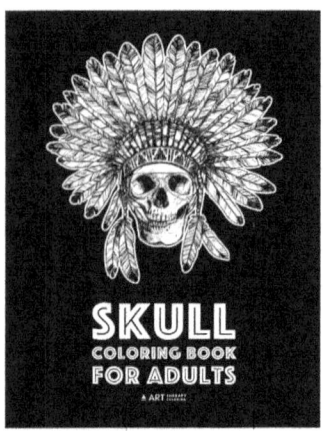

SKULL
COLORING BOOK
FOR ADULTS

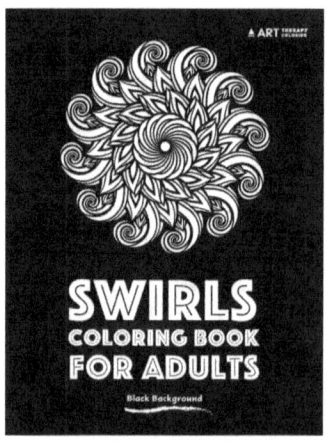

SWIRLS
COLORING BOOK
FOR ADULTS
Black Background

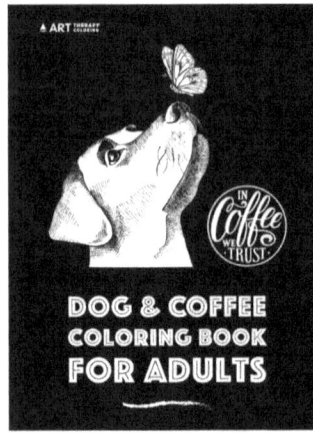

DOG & COFFEE
COLORING BOOK
FOR ADULTS

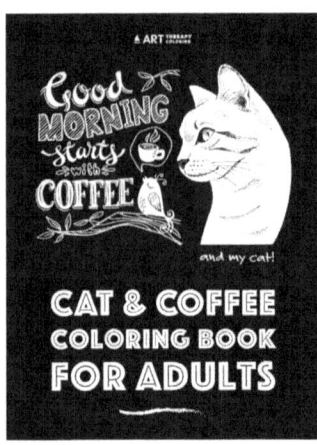

CAT & COFFEE
COLORING BOOK
FOR ADULTS

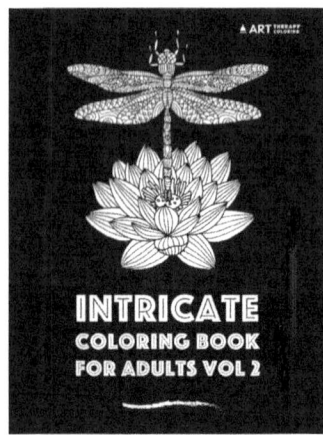

INTRICATE
COLORING BOOK
FOR ADULTS VOL 2

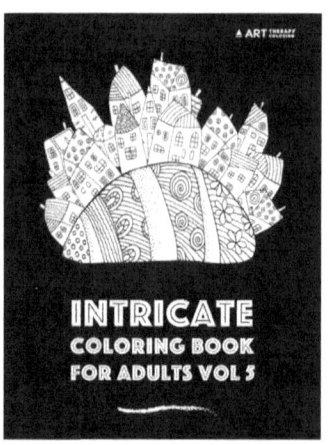

INTRICATE
COLORING BOOK
FOR ADULTS VOL 5

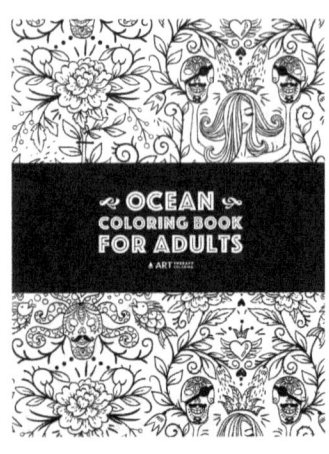

OCEAN
COLORING BOOK
FOR ADULTS

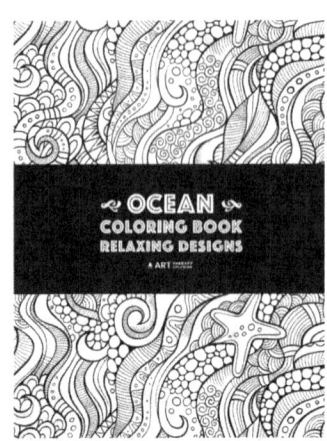

OCEAN
COLORING BOOK
RELAXING DESIGNS

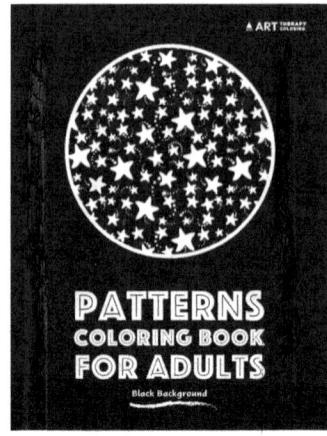

PATTERNS
COLORING BOOK
FOR ADULTS
Black Background

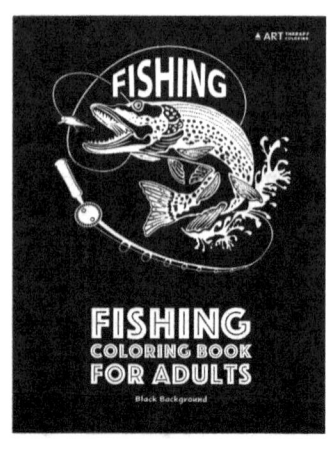

FISHING
COLORING BOOK
FOR ADULTS
Black Background

Coloring Books For Adults

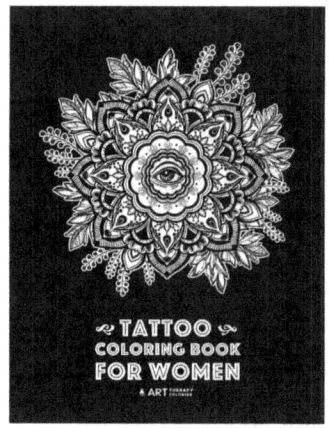

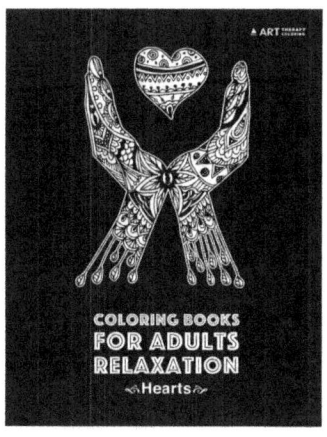

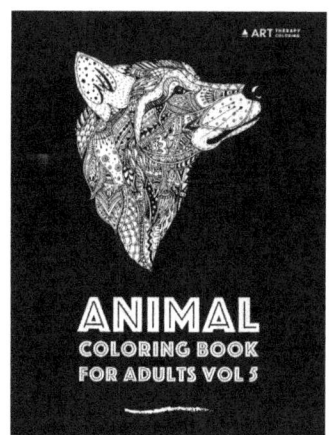

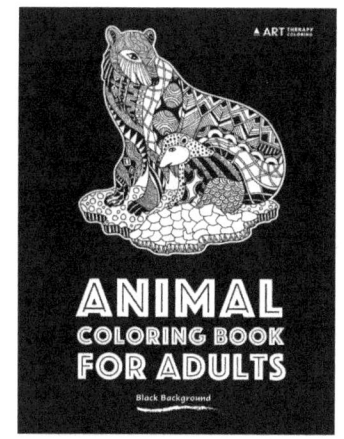

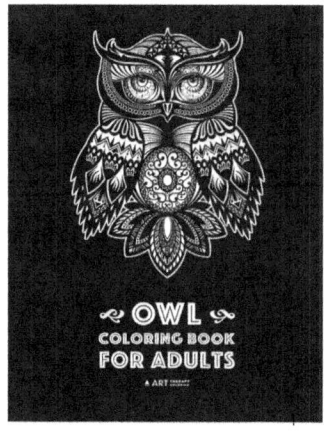

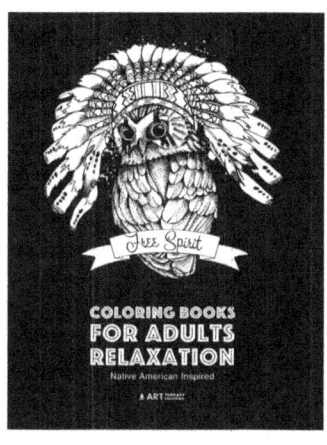

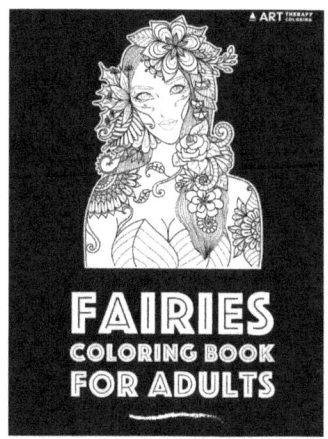

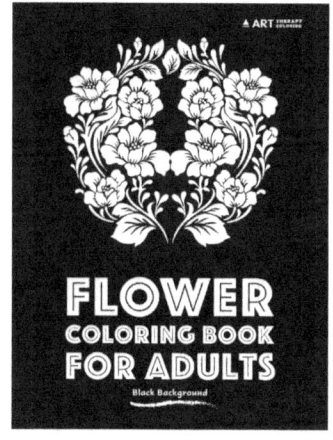

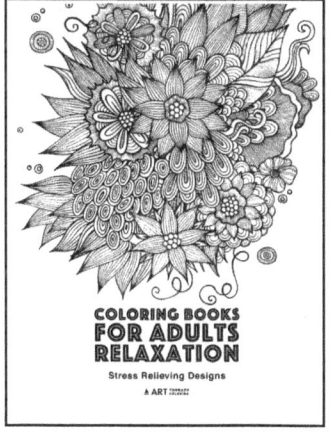

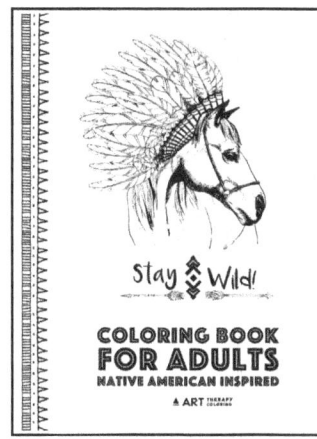

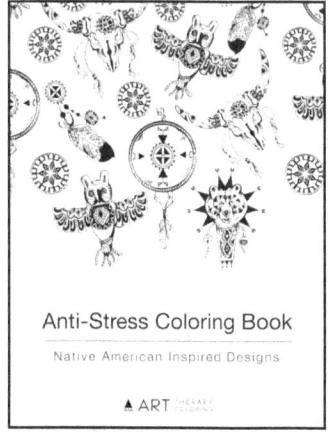

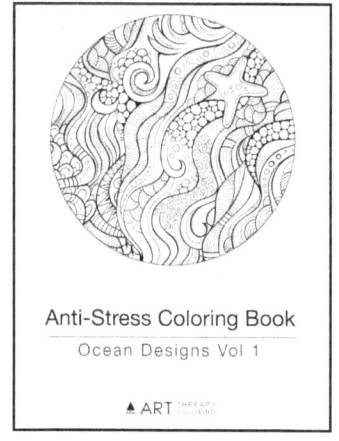

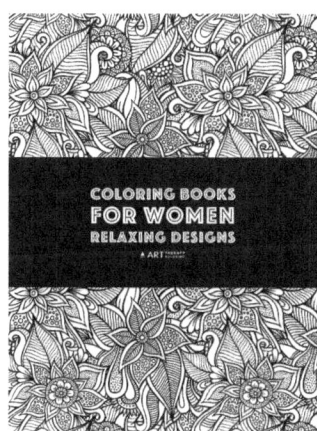

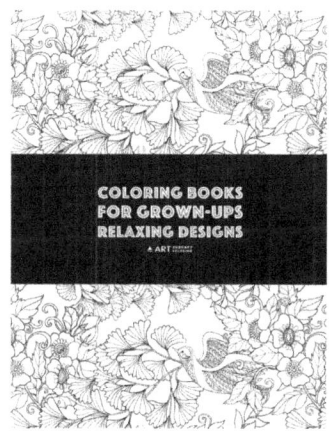

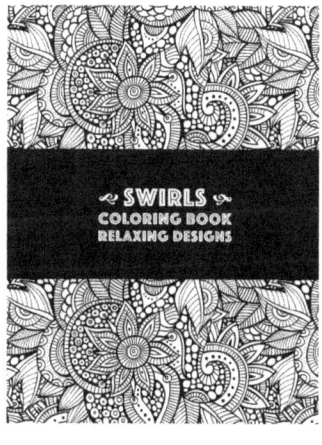

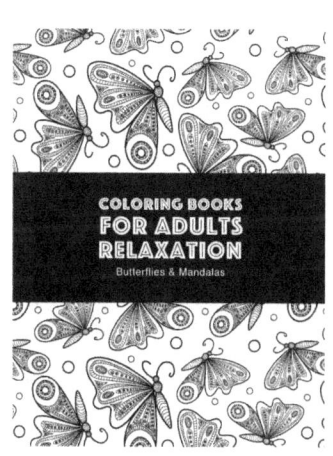

Coloring Books For Men

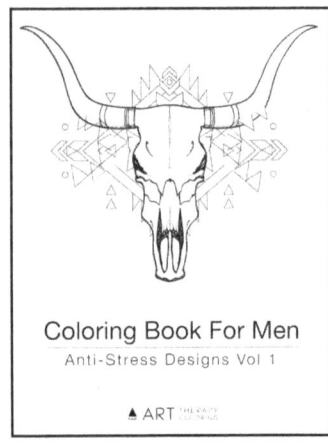

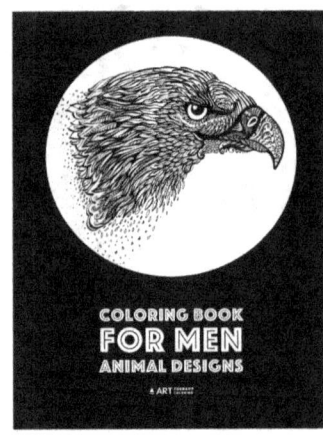

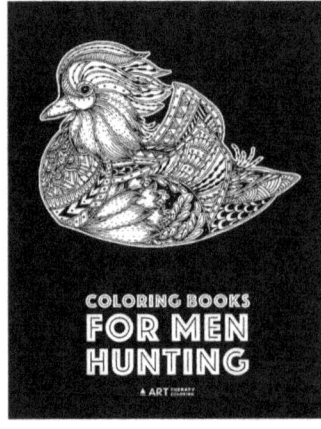

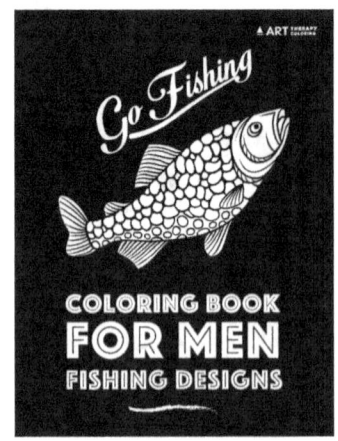

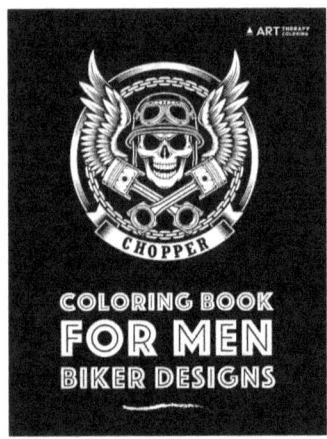

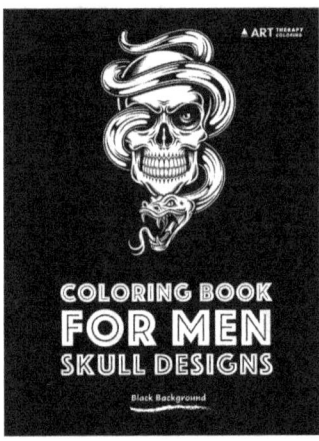

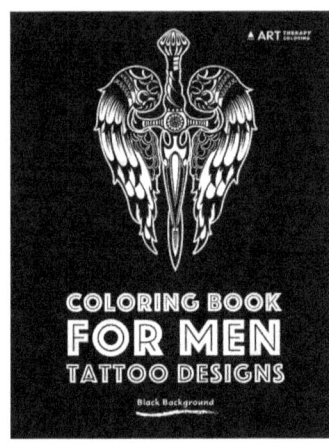

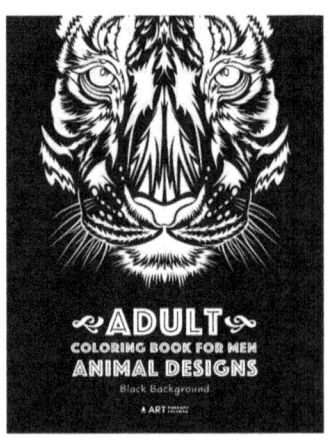

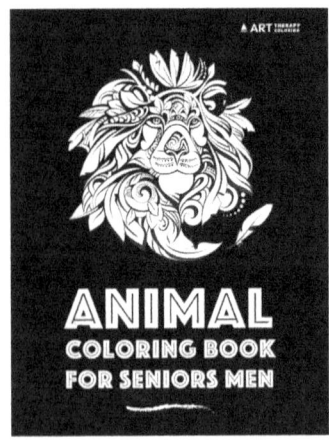

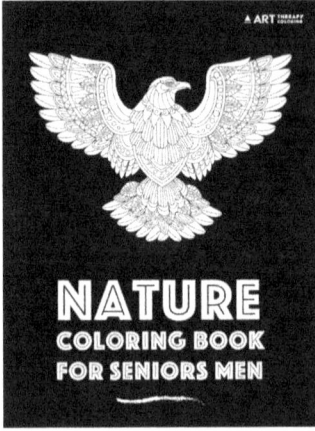

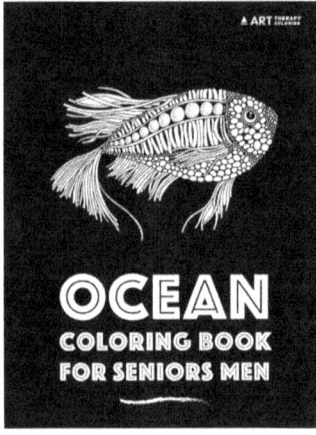

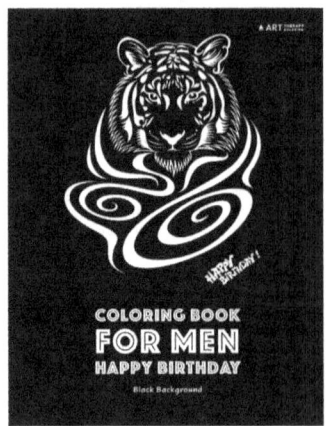

Coloring Books For Seniors

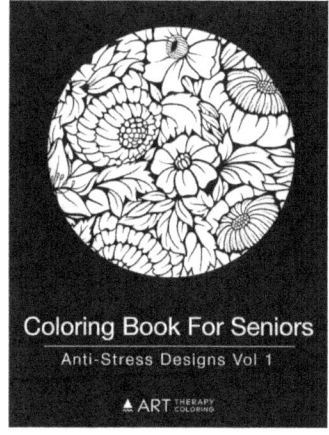

Coloring Book For Seniors
Anti-Stress Designs Vol 1

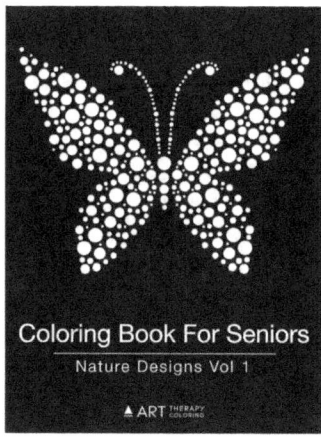

Coloring Book For Seniors
Nature Designs Vol 1

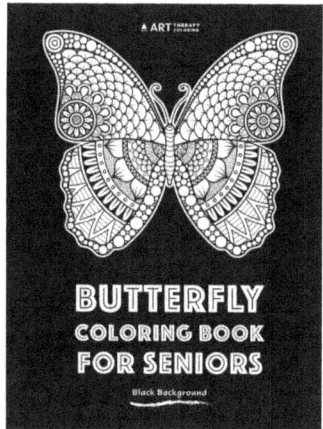

BUTTERFLY
COLORING BOOK
FOR SENIORS
Black Background

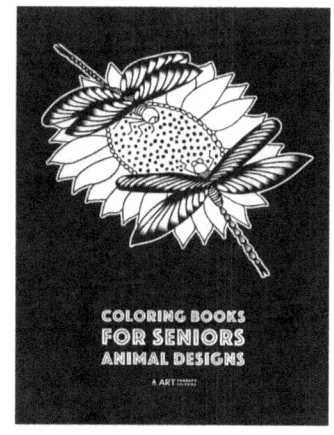

COLORING BOOKS
FOR SENIORS
ANIMAL DESIGNS

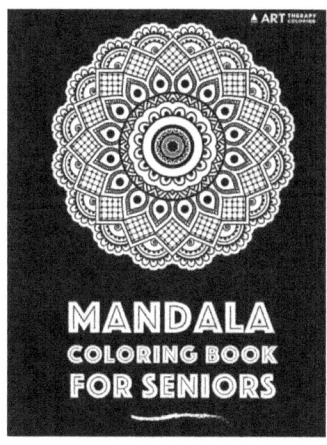

MANDALA
COLORING BOOK
FOR SENIORS
Black Background

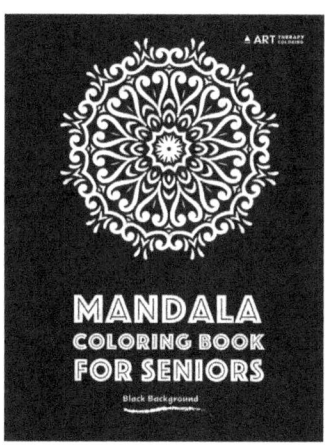

MANDALA
COLORING BOOK
FOR SENIORS
Black Background

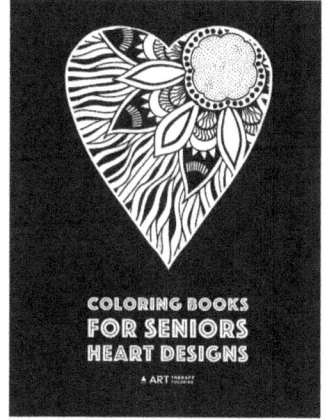

COLORING BOOKS
FOR SENIORS
HEART DESIGNS

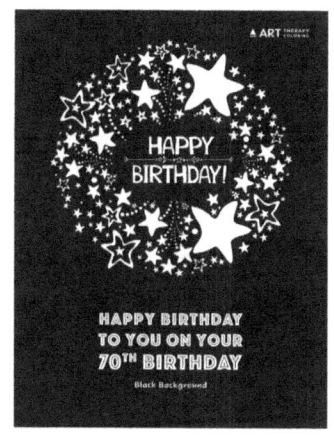

HAPPY BIRTHDAY
TO YOU ON YOUR
70TH BIRTHDAY
Black Background

COLORING BOOKS
FOR SENIORS
SWIRL DESIGNS
Black Background

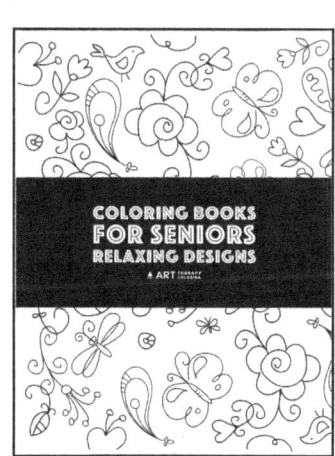

COLORING BOOKS
FOR SENIORS
RELAXING DESIGNS

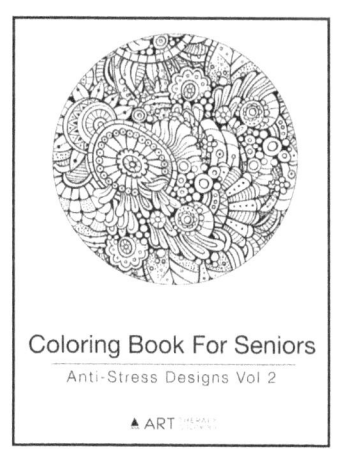

Coloring Book For Seniors
Anti-Stress Designs Vol 2

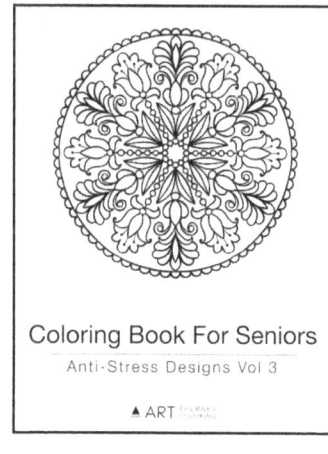

Coloring Book For Seniors
Anti-Stress Designs Vol 3

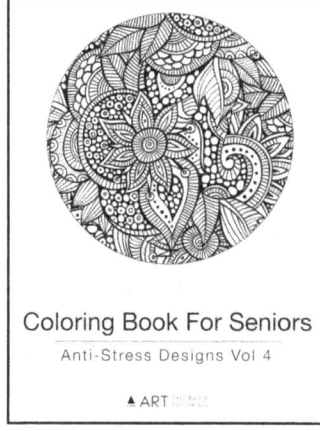

Coloring Book For Seniors
Anti-Stress Designs Vol 4

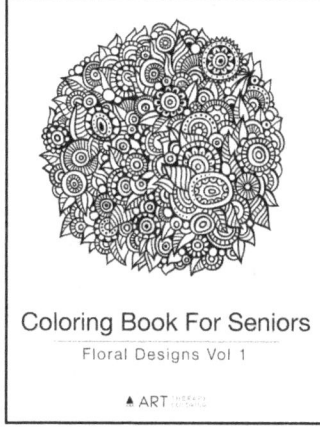

Coloring Book For Seniors
Floral Designs Vol 1

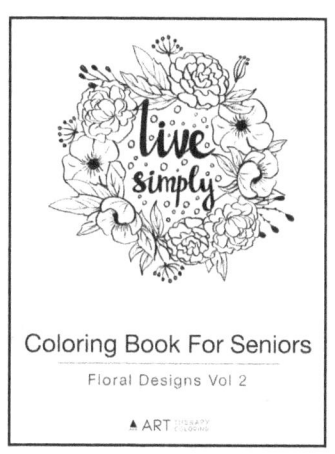

Coloring Book For Seniors
Floral Designs Vol 2

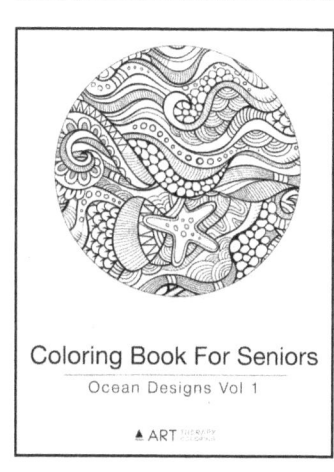

Coloring Book For Seniors
Ocean Designs Vol 1

Coloring Books For Teens

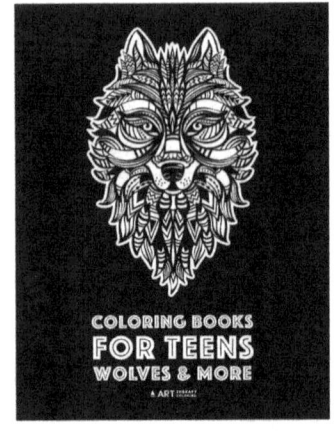

COLORING BOOKS
FOR TEENS
WOLVES & MORE
▲ ART THERAPY COLORING

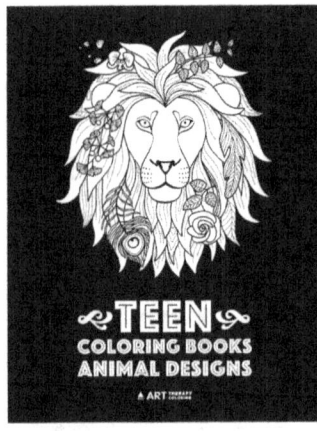

TEEN
COLORING BOOKS
ANIMAL DESIGNS
▲ ART THERAPY COLORING

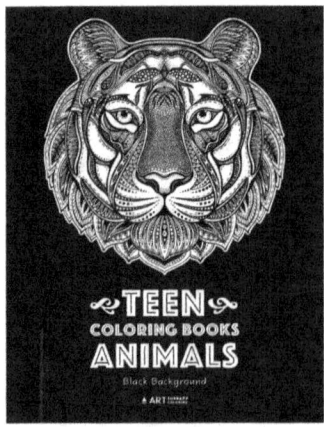

TEEN
COLORING BOOKS
ANIMALS
Black Background
▲ ART THERAPY COLORING

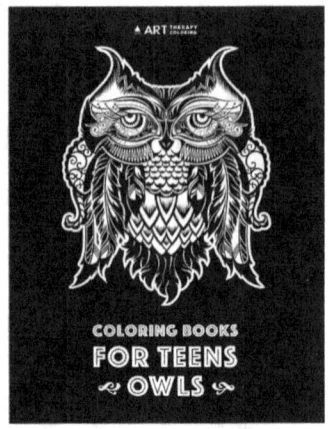

▲ ART THERAPY COLORING
COLORING BOOKS
FOR TEENS
OWLS

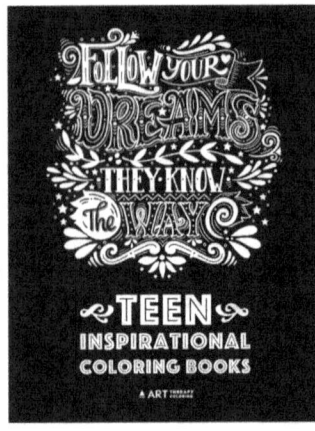

Follow your DREAMS THEY KNOW The WAY
TEEN
INSPIRATIONAL
COLORING BOOKS
▲ ART THERAPY COLORING

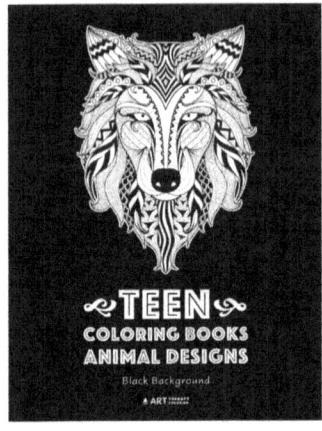

TEEN
COLORING BOOKS
ANIMAL DESIGNS
Black Background
▲ ART THERAPY COLORING

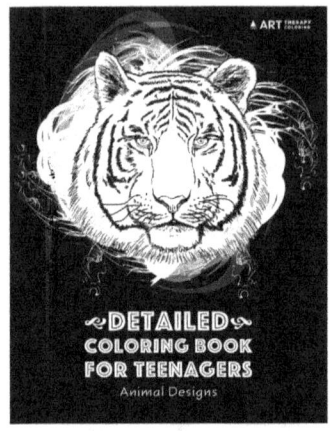

▲ ART THERAPY COLORING
DETAILED
COLORING BOOK
FOR TEENAGERS
Animal Designs

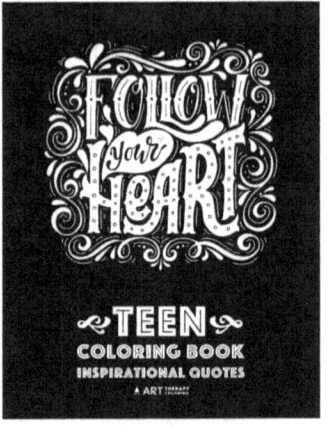

Follow your HEART
TEEN
COLORING BOOK
INSPIRATIONAL QUOTES
▲ ART THERAPY COLORING

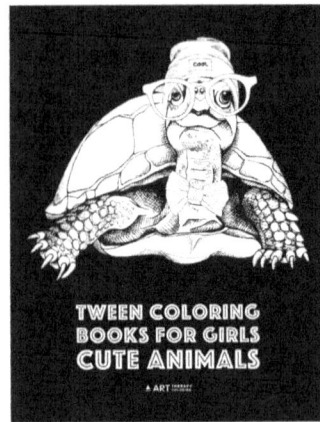

TWEEN COLORING
BOOKS FOR GIRLS
CUTE ANIMALS
▲ ART THERAPY COLORING

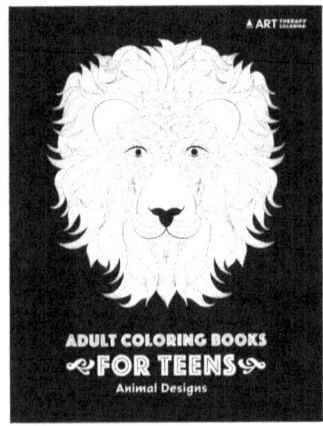

▲ ART THERAPY COLORING
ADULT COLORING BOOKS
FOR TEENS
Animal Designs

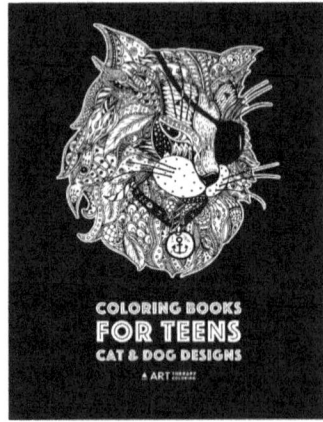

COLORING BOOKS
FOR TEENS
CAT & DOG DESIGNS
▲ ART THERAPY COLORING

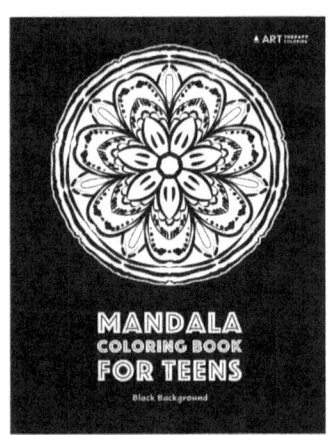

▲ ART THERAPY COLORING
MANDALA
COLORING BOOK
FOR TEENS
Black Background

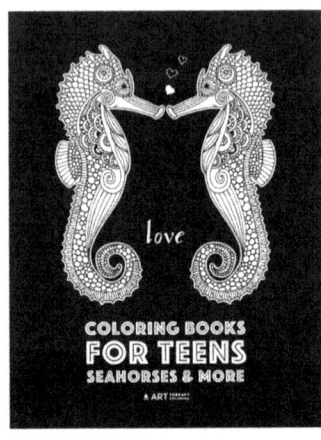

love
COLORING BOOKS
FOR TEENS
SEAHORSES & MORE
▲ ART THERAPY COLORING

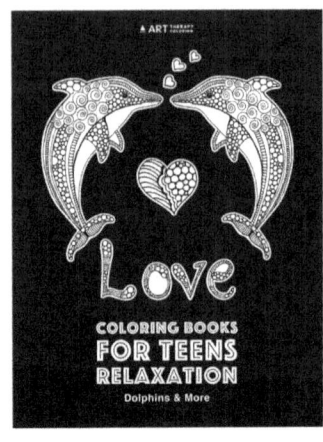

▲ ART THERAPY COLORING
Love
COLORING BOOKS
FOR TEENS
RELAXATION
Dolphins & More

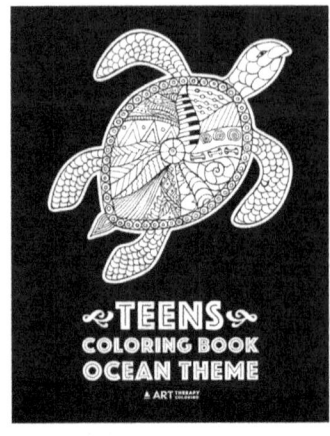

TEENS
COLORING BOOK
OCEAN THEME
▲ ART THERAPY COLORING

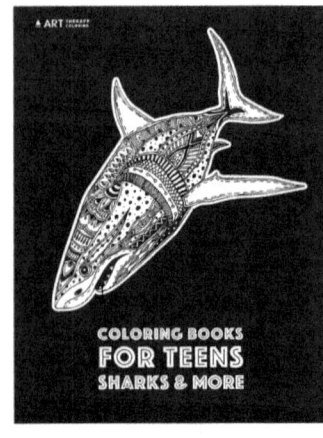

▲ ART THERAPY COLORING
COLORING BOOKS
FOR TEENS
SHARKS & MORE

Coloring Books For Teens

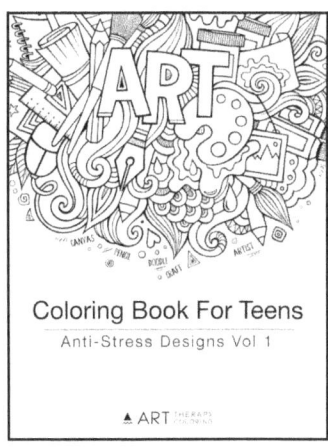

Coloring Book For Teens
Anti-Stress Designs Vol 1

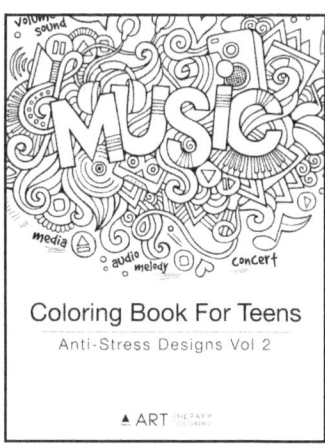

Coloring Book For Teens
Anti-Stress Designs Vol 2

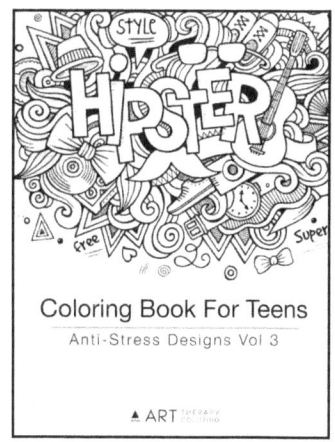

Coloring Book For Teens
Anti-Stress Designs Vol 3

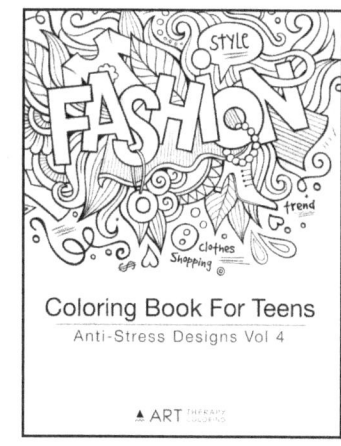

Coloring Book For Teens
Anti-Stress Designs Vol 4

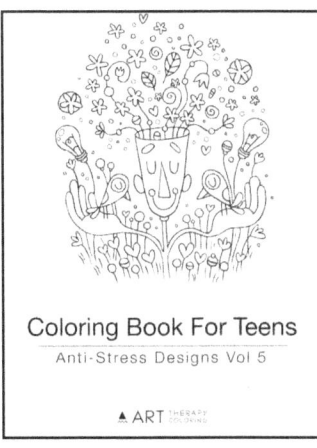

Coloring Book For Teens
Anti-Stress Designs Vol 5

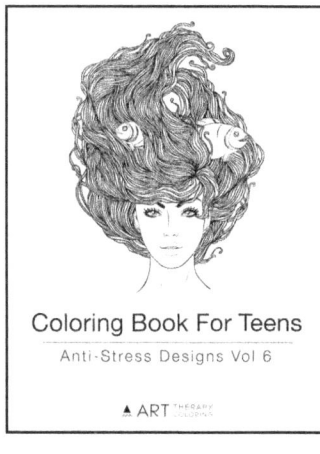

Coloring Book For Teens
Anti-Stress Designs Vol 6

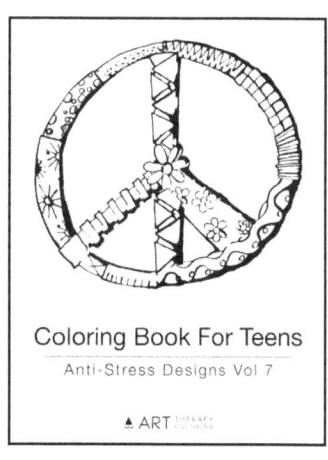

Coloring Book For Teens
Anti-Stress Designs Vol 7

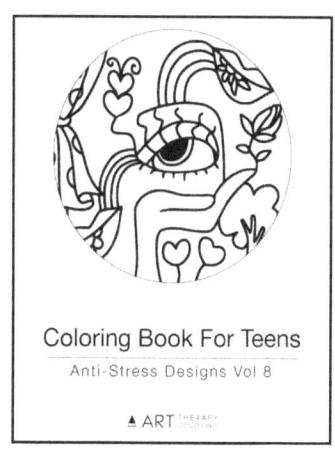

Coloring Book For Teens
Anti-Stress Designs Vol 8

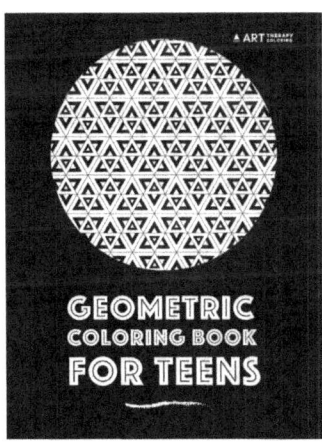

GEOMETRIC COLORING BOOK FOR TEENS

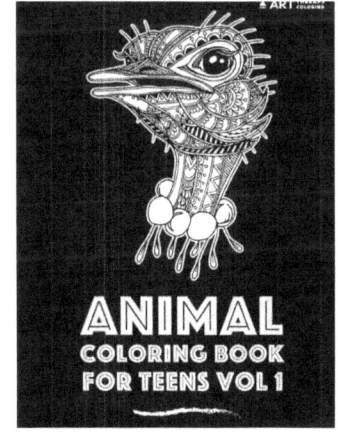

ANIMAL COLORING BOOK FOR TEENS VOL 1

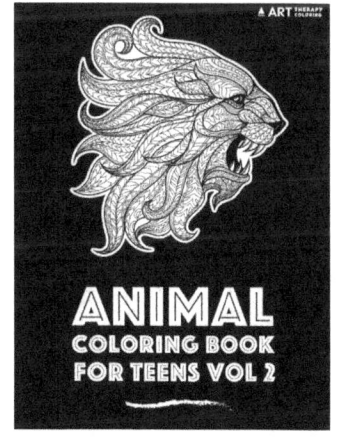

ANIMAL COLORING BOOK FOR TEENS VOL 2

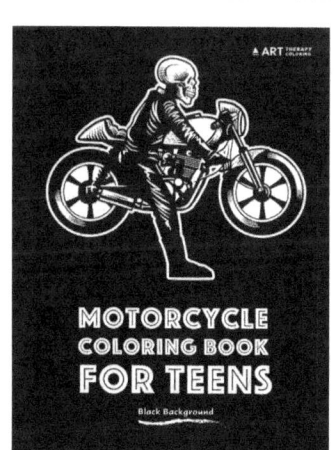

MOTORCYCLE COLORING BOOK FOR TEENS
Black Background

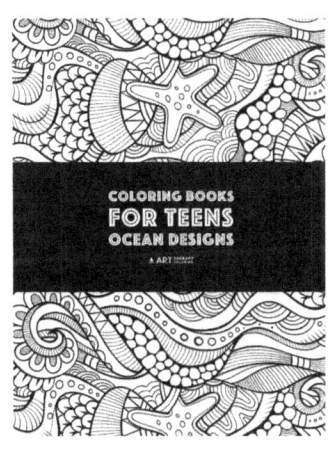

COLORING BOOKS FOR TEENS OCEAN DESIGNS

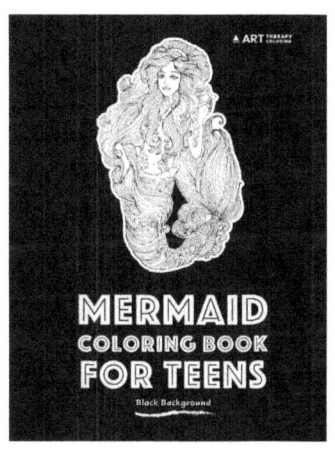

MERMAID COLORING BOOK FOR TEENS
Black Background

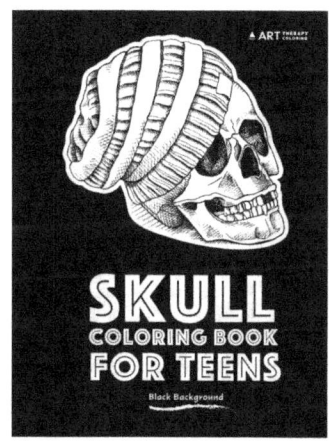

SKULL COLORING BOOK FOR TEENS
Black Background

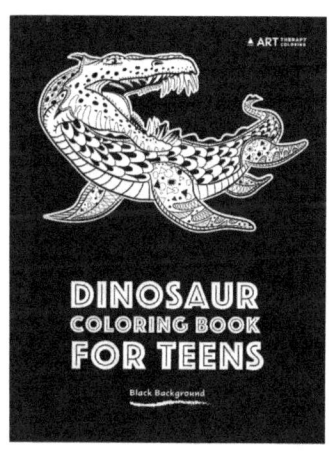

DINOSAUR COLORING BOOK FOR TEENS
Black Background

Coloring Books For Girls

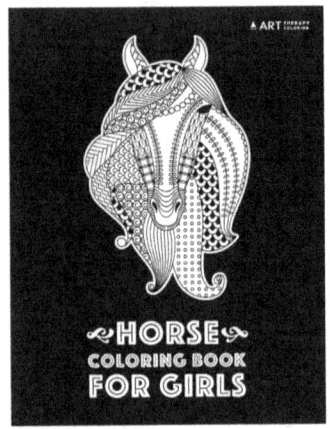

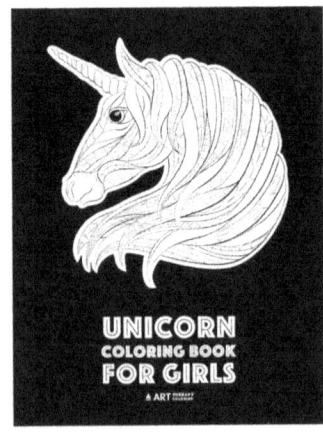

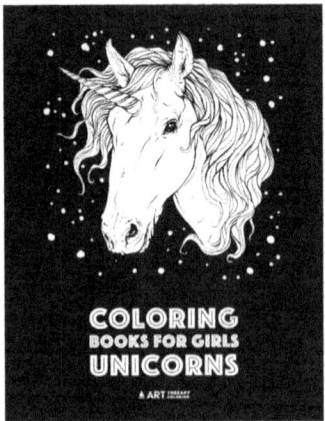

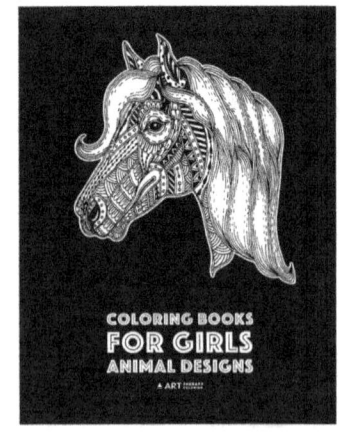

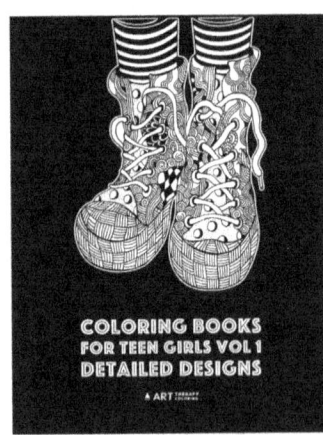

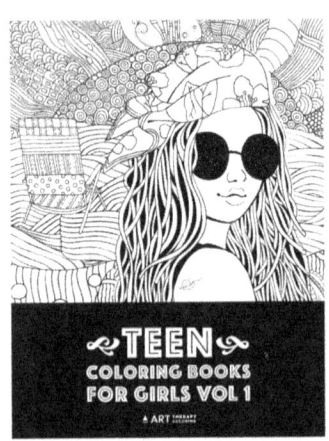

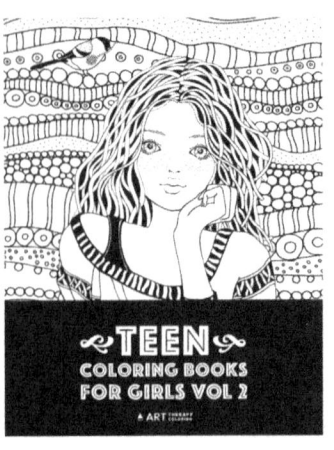

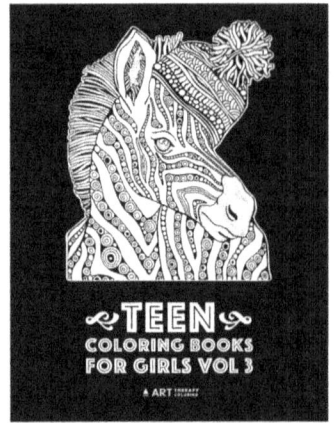

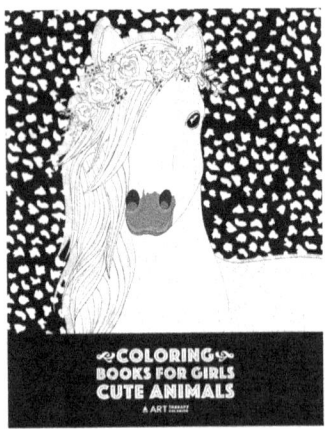

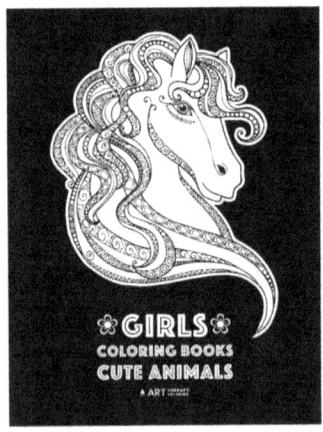

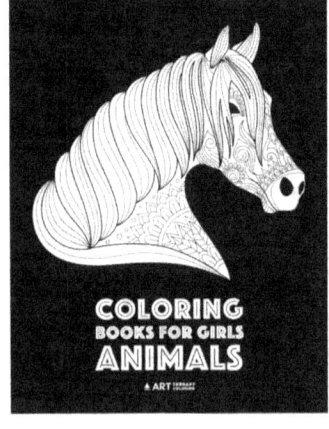

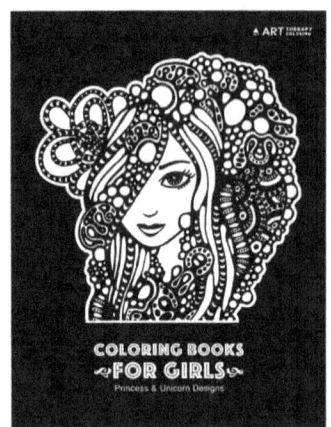

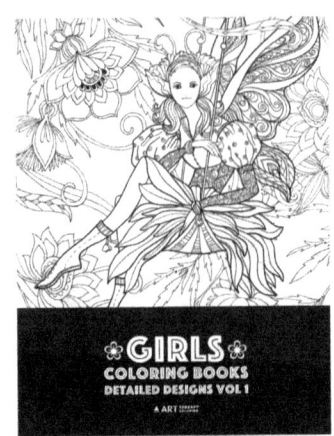

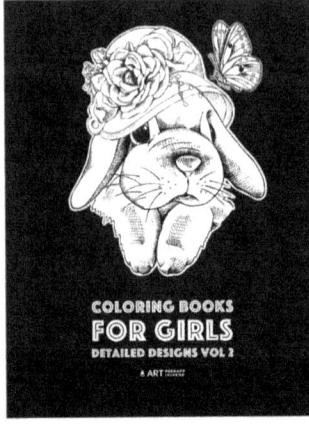

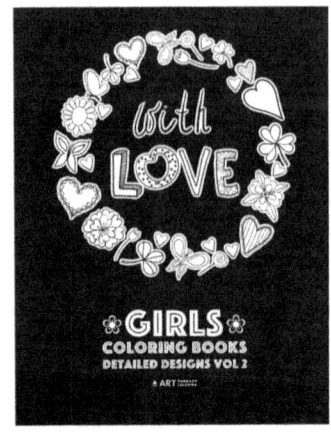

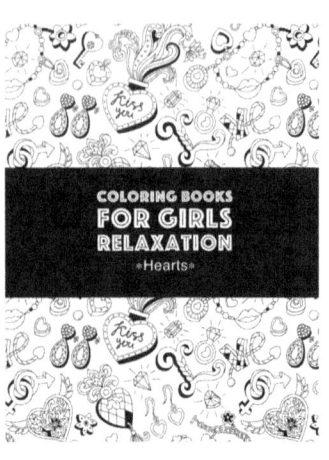

Art Therapy Coloring Books

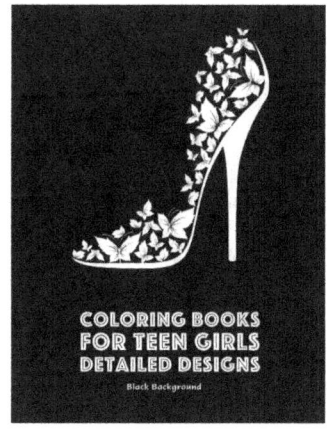

COLORING BOOKS
FOR TEEN GIRLS
DETAILED DESIGNS
Black Background

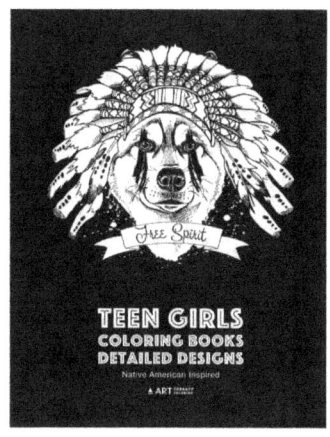

TEEN GIRLS
COLORING BOOKS
DETAILED DESIGNS
Native American Inspired

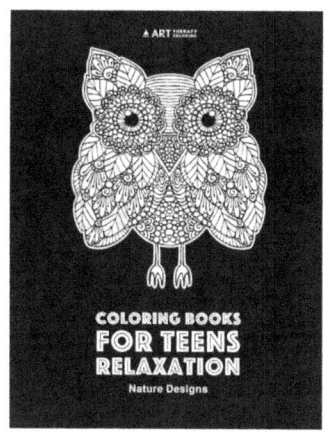

COLORING BOOKS
FOR TEENS
RELAXATION
Nature Designs

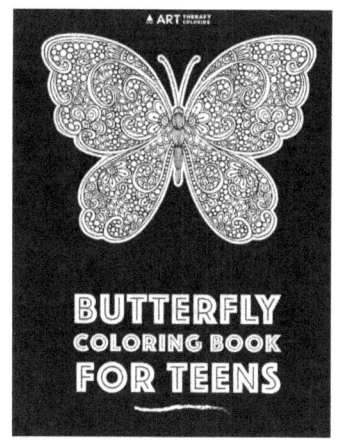

BUTTERFLY
COLORING BOOK
FOR TEENS

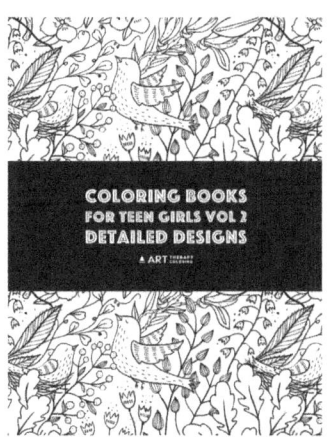

COLORING BOOKS
FOR TEEN GIRLS VOL 2
DETAILED DESIGNS

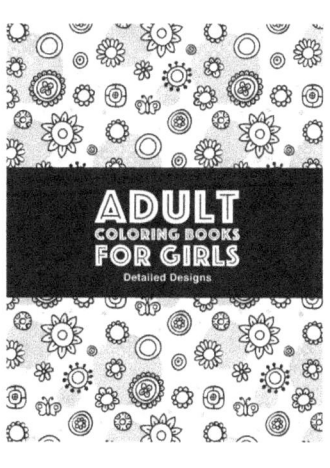

ADULT
COLORING BOOKS
FOR GIRLS
Detailed Designs

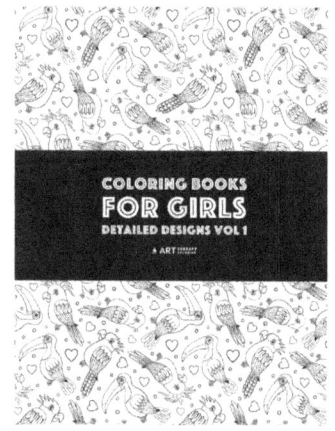

COLORING BOOKS
FOR GIRLS
DETAILED DESIGNS VOL 1

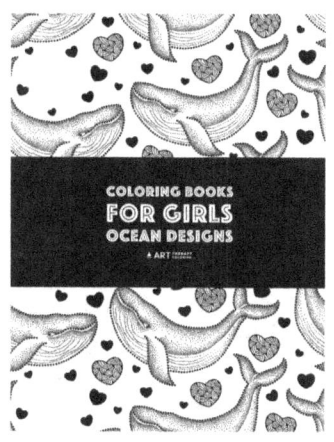

COLORING BOOKS
FOR GIRLS
OCEAN DESIGNS

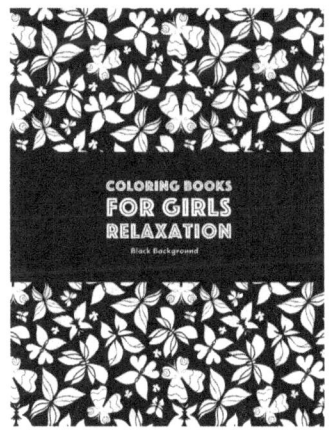

COLORING BOOKS
FOR GIRLS
RELAXATION
Black Background

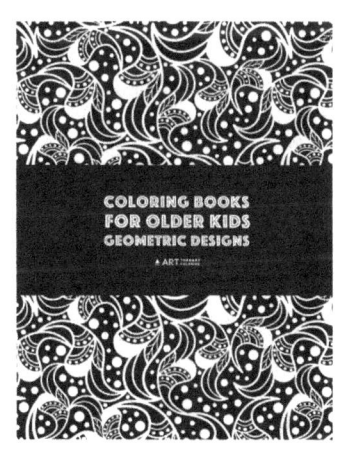

COLORING BOOKS
FOR OLDER KIDS
GEOMETRIC DESIGNS

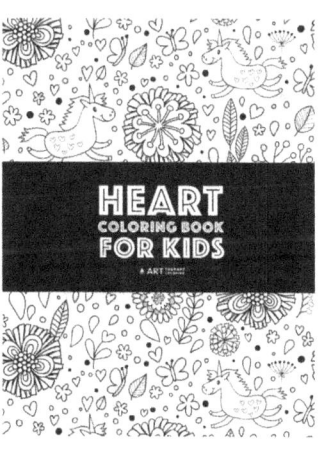

HEART
COLORING BOOK
FOR KIDS

DETAILED
COLORING BOOKS
FOR KIDS
Ocean Designs

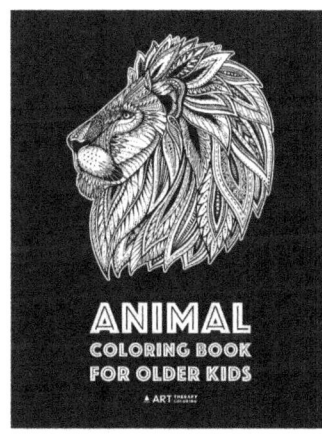

ANIMAL
COLORING BOOK
FOR OLDER KIDS

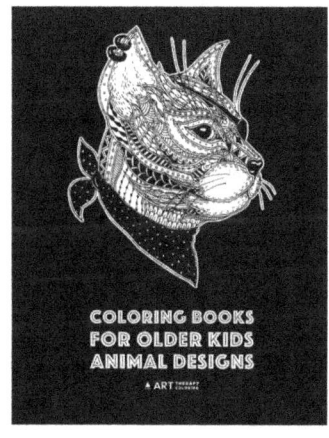

COLORING BOOKS
FOR OLDER KIDS
ANIMAL DESIGNS

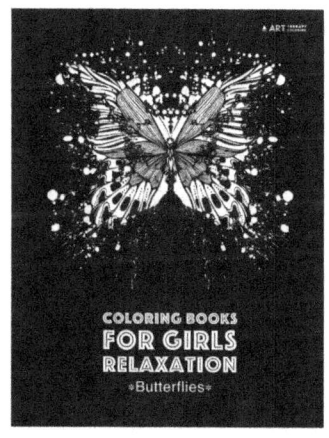

COLORING BOOKS
FOR GIRLS
RELAXATION
Butterflies

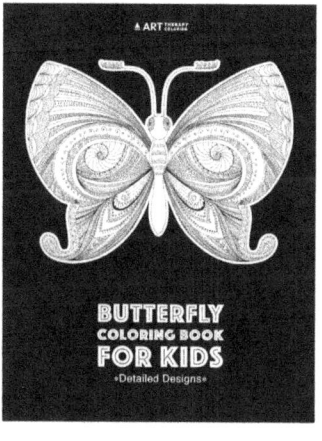

BUTTERFLY
COLORING BOOK
FOR KIDS
Detailed Designs

Coloring Books For Boys

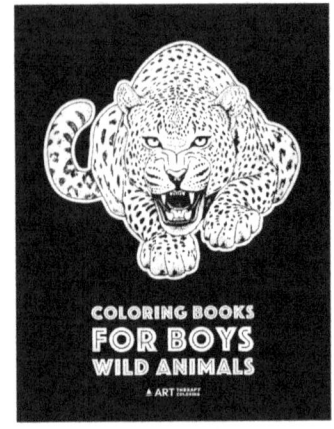

COLORING BOOKS
FOR BOYS
WILD ANIMALS
ART THERAPY COLORING

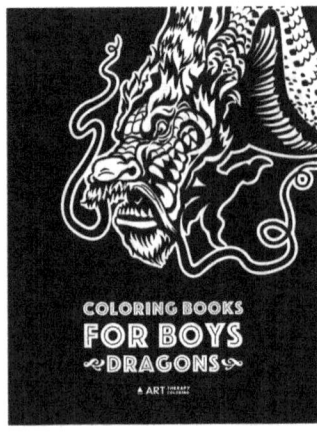

COLORING BOOKS
FOR BOYS
~DRAGONS~
ART THERAPY COLORING

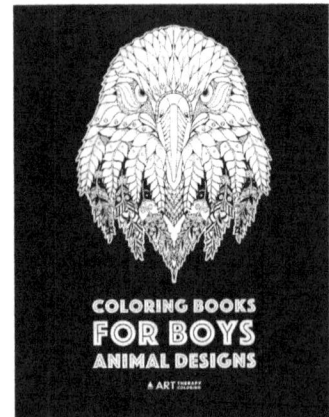

COLORING BOOKS
FOR BOYS
ANIMAL DESIGNS
ART THERAPY COLORING

COLORING BOOKS
FOR BOYS
OCEAN DESIGNS
Black Background

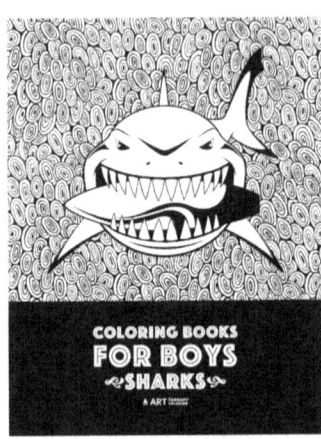

COLORING BOOKS
FOR BOYS
~SHARKS~
ART THERAPY COLORING

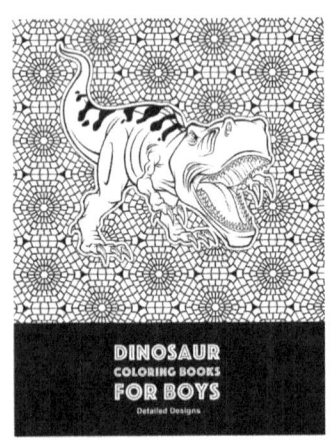

DINOSAUR
COLORING BOOKS
FOR BOYS
Detailed Designs

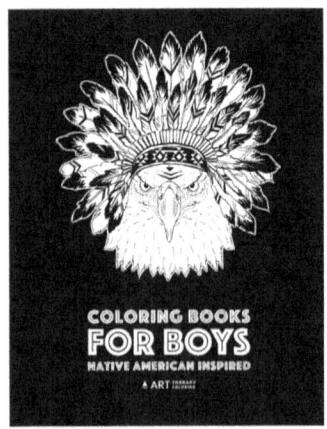

COLORING BOOKS
FOR BOYS
NATIVE AMERICAN INSPIRED
ART THERAPY COLORING

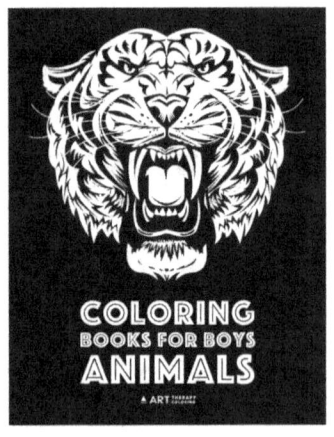

COLORING
BOOKS FOR BOYS
ANIMALS
ART THERAPY COLORING

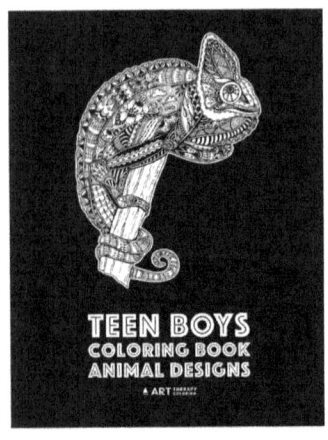

TEEN BOYS
COLORING BOOK
ANIMAL DESIGNS
ART THERAPY COLORING

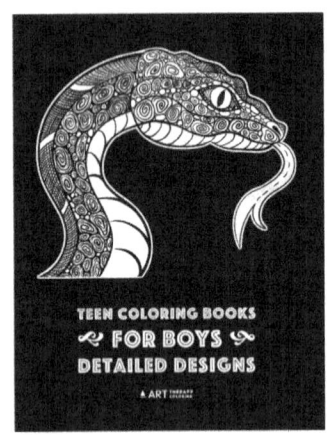

TEEN COLORING BOOKS
~ FOR BOYS ~
DETAILED DESIGNS
ART THERAPY COLORING

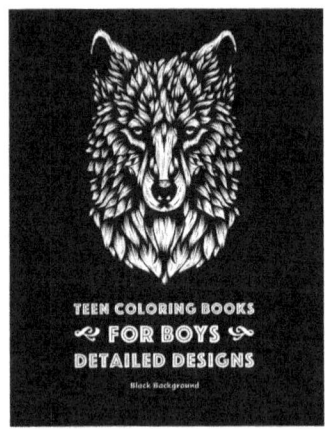

TEEN COLORING BOOKS
~ FOR BOYS ~
DETAILED DESIGNS
Black Background

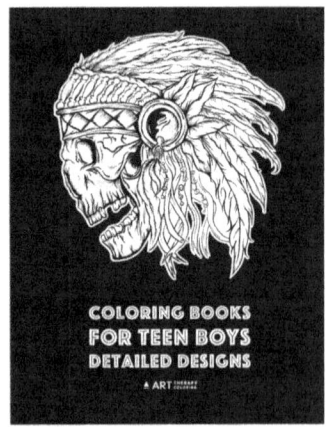

COLORING BOOKS
FOR TEEN BOYS
DETAILED DESIGNS

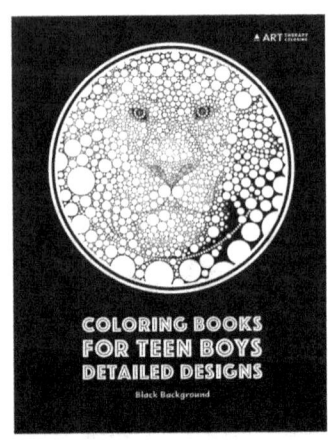

COLORING BOOKS
FOR TEEN BOYS
DETAILED DESIGNS
Black Background

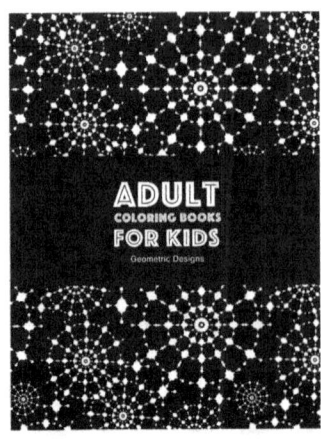

ADULT
COLORING BOOKS
FOR KIDS
Geometric Designs

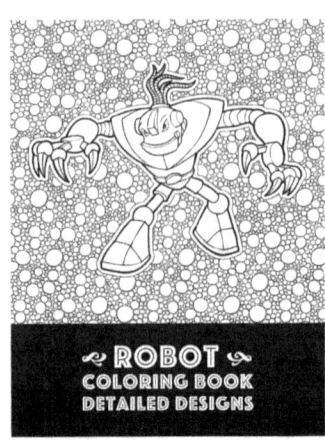

~ ROBOT ~
COLORING BOOK
DETAILED DESIGNS

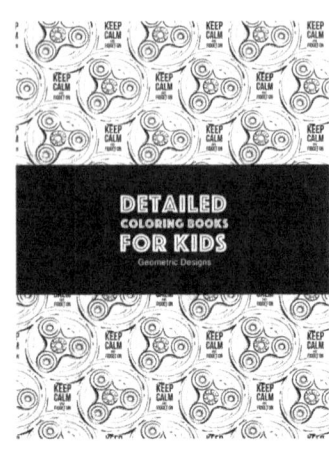

DETAILED
COLORING BOOKS
FOR KIDS
Geometric Designs

Coloring Books For Kids

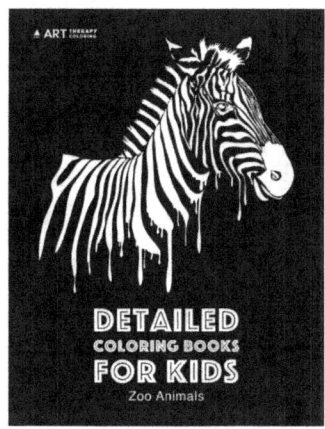

DETAILED COLORING BOOKS **FOR KIDS**
Zoo Animals

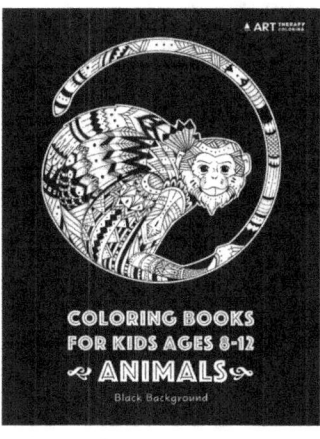

COLORING BOOKS FOR KIDS AGES 8-12 ~ANIMALS~
Black Background

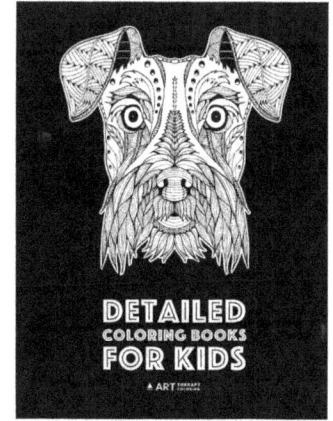

DETAILED COLORING BOOKS **FOR KIDS**

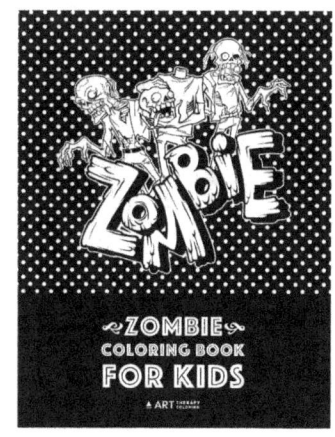

~ZOMBIE~ COLORING BOOK **FOR KIDS**

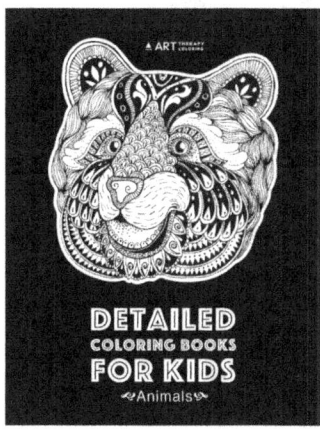

DETAILED COLORING BOOKS **FOR KIDS** ~Animals~

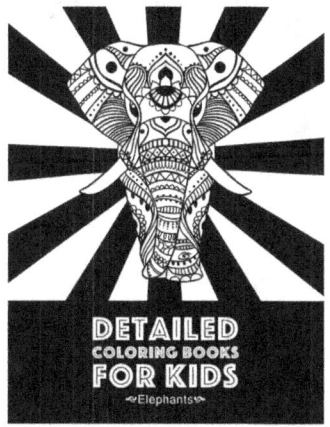

DETAILED COLORING BOOKS **FOR KIDS** ~Elephants~

COLORING BOOKS **FOR KIDS** OCEAN DESIGNS

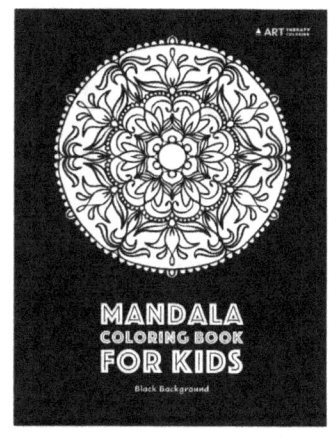

MANDALA COLORING BOOK **FOR KIDS**
Black Background

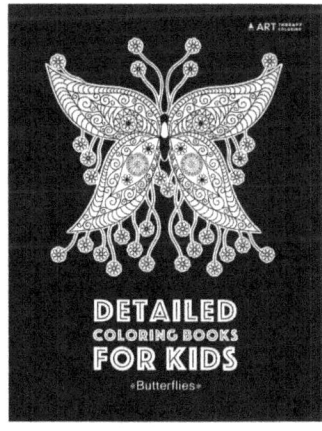

DETAILED COLORING BOOKS **FOR KIDS** ~Butterflies~

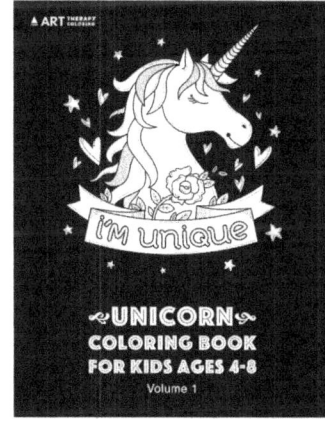

~UNICORN~ COLORING BOOK **FOR KIDS AGES 4-8**
Volume 1

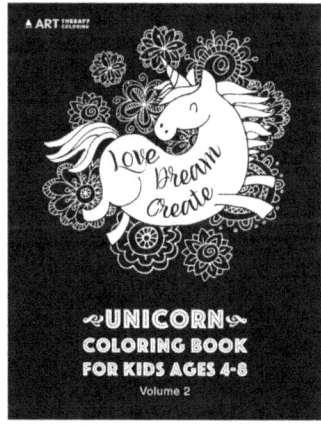

~UNICORN~ COLORING BOOK **FOR KIDS AGES 4-8**
Volume 2

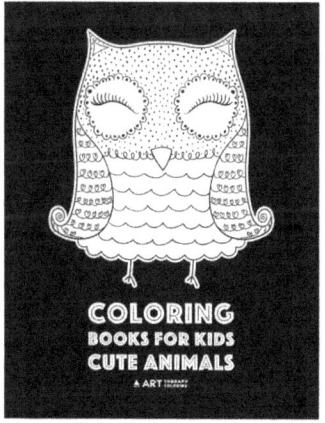

COLORING BOOKS FOR KIDS CUTE ANIMALS

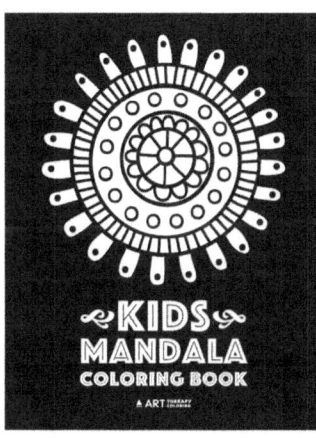

~KIDS~ **MANDALA** COLORING BOOK

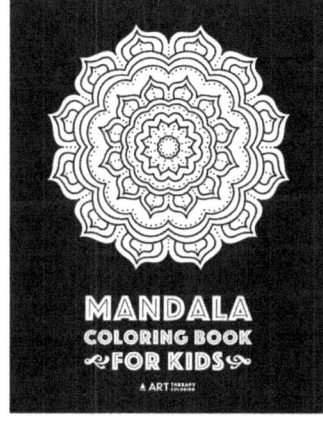

MANDALA COLORING BOOK ~FOR KIDS~

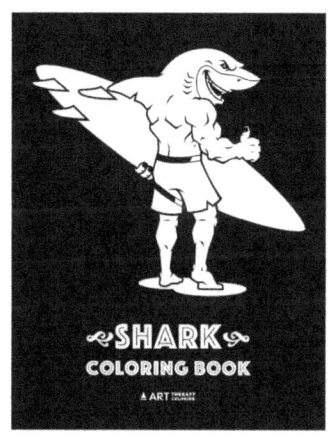

~SHARK~ COLORING BOOK

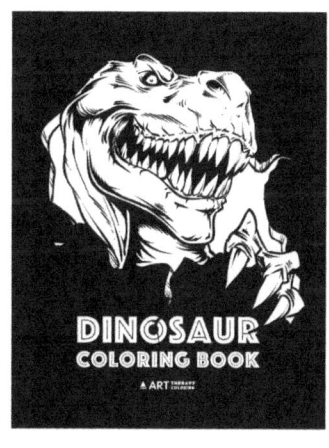

DINOSAUR COLORING BOOK

Coloring Books For Special Occasions

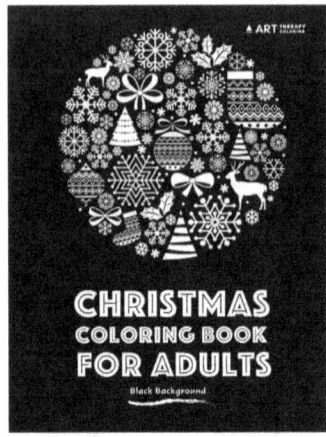

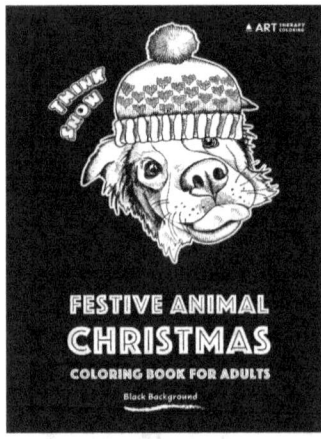

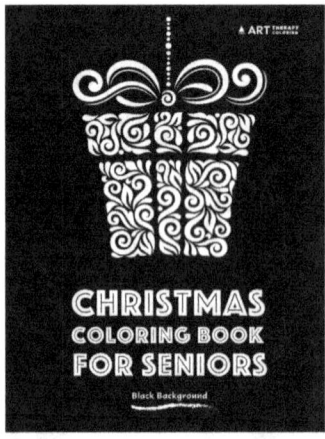

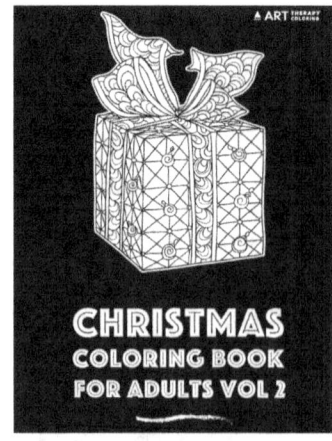

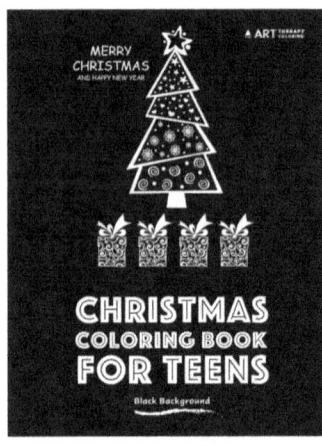

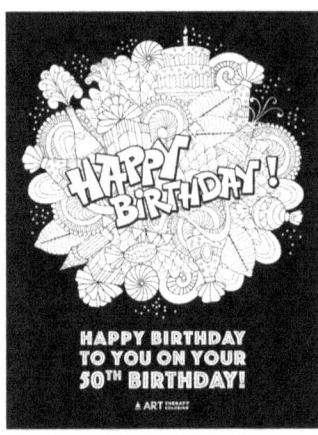

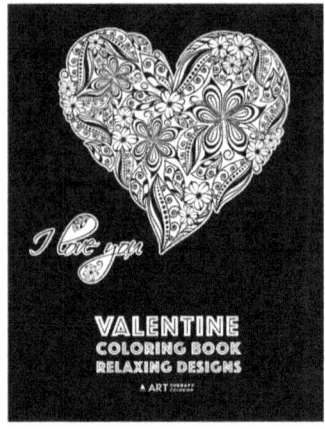

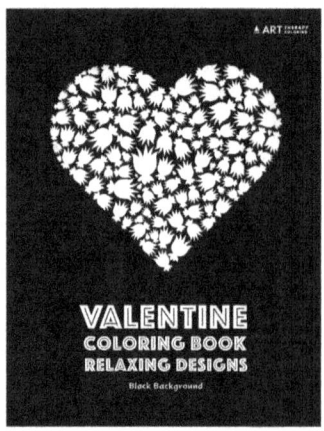

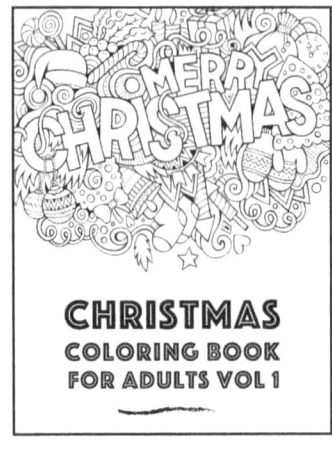

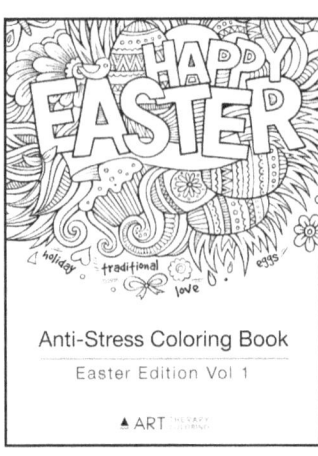

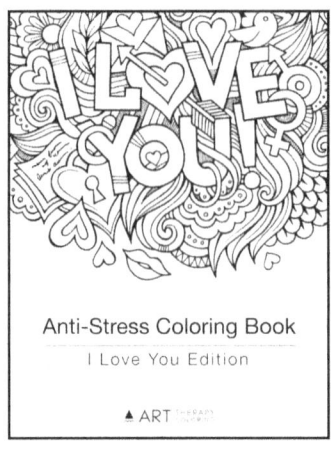

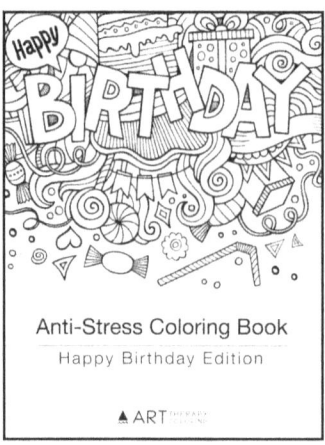

Lion Coloring Book For Adults

Published by:
Art Therapy Coloring
El Dorado Hills, California
www.arttherapycoloring.com

Shutterstock Images

ISBN: 978-1-64126-013-8

www.ingramcontent.com/pod-product-compliance
Lightning Source LLC
Chambersburg PA
CBHW081240180526
45171CB00005B/487